London
Transport

in the 1940s

Ian Allan
PUBLISHING

Michael H. C. Baker

Contents

Front cover: 'Feltham' tram No 2103 heads through Streatham on its way from the Embankment to Purley. The story of London's trams might have been very different had this revolutionary design, introduced by the MET and LUT companies in the early 1930s, been perpetuated by London Transport; the 'Felthams' were fast, more comfortable than any contemporary motor bus and immensely popular with passengers, crews, engineers and management alike. *C. Carter*

Back cover: Tottenham High Road shortly after the end of a Tottenham Hotspur home match. Although this is a postwar picture the scene would have been much the same at any time in the trolleybus era. There are at least 15 trolleybuses in view and one solitary motor bus (a wartime Guy). Shepherded by the police, the crowds wait patiently on this wet Saturday afternoon whilst shoppers go about their business. *London Transport*

Title page: Fleet Street, looking towards Ludgate Circus and St Paul's. Amongst the STLs are two RTs; that heading away from the camera has the white spot applied to motor buses during the blackout and which, for some reason, was painted on the early RTs, although, even more curiously, the following STL, still in wartime livery, does not have it. *London Transport*

First published 2003

ISBN 0 7110 2918 0

Published by Ian Allan Publishing
an imprint of Ian Allan Publishing Ltd, Hersham, Surrey KT12 4RG.
Printed by Ian Allan Printing Ltd, Hersham, Surrey KT12 4RG.

Code: 0305/B

Introduction

THERE was never a more traumatic decade in London's varied and often violent history than that which began in 1940. Following the declaration of World War 2 in September 1939, much upheaval had been caused to the lives and travelling habits of Londoners, but this was as nothing compared to that which would occur when the Blitz was unleashed upon the capital at the end of the summer of 1940.

Almost my earliest memory is of sitting under our huge, old wooden kitchen table and saying to my mother: 'It's 1940 now, isn't it?' As I was 2½ years old at the time I don't imagine the concept of years passing would have meant very much, but something on the radio, or perhaps a conversation between my parents, must have taken sufficient hold of my infant sensibilities for the passing of the 1930s to have registered.

As far as transport in London was concerned the 1930s were scarcely less dramatic than the 1940s, although marked by great progress rather than by destruction and tragedy. The London Passenger Transport Board, known to all as London Transport, came into existence a third of the way through the decade, on Saturday 1 July 1933. A curious day to choose, Saturday. Inevitably, few passengers — or anyone else in the London Transport operating area of some 2,000 square miles — would have noticed anything different about the bus, coach, tram, trolleybus or train which took them to work and brought them home again on that first day. And remember that in 1933 a great many people did work on a Saturday, usually until lunchtime. On the back of the 1937 issue of the Central Area bus map, under the heading 'Standing passengers', one reads

Tram conductors studying notices at their desks in the modernised depot at Finchley, shortly before trolleybuses were allocated there. Behind are the counter where takings were handed in and clocks showing the headway of services; similar recorders were on view to the public at London Transport Headquarters, 55 Broadway, during the tram and trolleybus eras. *London Transport*

that up to five were allowed during the morning and evening rush hours, Monday to Friday, and 'Saturday up to 9.30am [and] between 12.30 and 2.30pm'. In 1948, on passing the Eleven-plus, I found myself attending school on Saturday morning, and many schoolchildren contributed to the heavy demand for public transport at lunchtime. Later in the day, tens of thousands of fans would make their way to the many professional football clubs in the London area. My own club, Crystal Palace (well, we all have a cross to bear), despite more than once finishing at the foot of the Third Division South, attracted so many masochists like myself that I usually walked the 2½ miles to the ground at Selhurst Park rather than attempt to board a 42 tram.

Practically everyone within London Transport's 2,000 square miles would have been a customer of London Transport, on either a regular or a casual basis, for relatively few people owned cars, and, even if you did, more than one per family was unheard of, unless you were amazingly rich. In 1939 500,000,000 journeys were made on LPTB's trains, buses, coaches, trams and trolleybuses.

The LPTB had just six years to stamp its mark on the transport scene in London and the Home Counties before being engulfed by war. But what use it made of those six years! It is no exaggeration to claim that by the summer of 1939 it was probably the most advanced transport undertaking of any size anywhere in the world. This was due chiefly to two men, although many others played their parts admirably. One was Lord Ashfield, the Chairman, the other Frank Pick, his deputy. They possessed many qualities, but above all it was their vision which ensured that, in terms of design, vehicles, buildings, posters and just about every aspect of its infrastructure, London Transport led the way.

The declaration of war on 3 September 1939 drastically curtailed this wonderful, surging energy but would not bring it to a grinding halt. The consolation was that the achievements of the 1930s and the standards reached enabled London Transport to cope as well as it did with all that was to beset it, not only during the war but also during the years of slow and painful recovery which followed, through the remainder of the 1940s and into the 1950s.

Neville Chamberlain — a decent, peace-loving man who had seen at first hand between 1914 and 1918 what horrors war could bring, and who did all he could to keep Britain out of any future conflict until he realised, too late, that Hitler could not be dealt with in terms that he (Chamberlain) could understand — declared war on Nazi Germany on Sunday 3 September, 1939. The crisis of the previous year, when Chamberlain had flown to Munich and had returned with his infamous 'piece of paper', signed by himself and Hitler, promising 'peace in our time', had brought home to practically everyone in Britain the inevitability of war. There is a picture in one of our family albums of me sitting on my father's knee in the back garden with the caption '1st shelter "Munich", 1938'. Those who had followed the maverick Conservative, Winston Churchill, who would succeed Chamberlain in 1940, knew Munich was only postponing the inevitable.

Thus London Transport was not unprepared. On 31 August 1939 — ahead of the official declaration of war — most Green Line services were withdrawn and, in an astonishingly few, short hours, the coaches converted to ambulances. The general expectation, fuelled by numerous writers of both fact and fiction and by cinema films, was that there would be immediate, devastating air attacks on British cities. Evacuation of schoolchildren and, to a limited extent, other civilians began, and by 5 September over half a million had been moved by London Transport, mostly to railway stations in the centre of the capital or the suburbs for long-distance travel onwards, but sometimes the buses or coaches would be used for the entire journey, to the coast or elsewhere. For those brought by the Underground, Edgware station on the Northern Line was the main departure point by road. When the expected invasion from the skies failed to materialise many drifted back home, but, with the fall of France in the summer of 1940, evacuation of children once again took place, this time in many cases for the duration of the war. Between 13 and 18 June 1940 111,000 London children and their attendants were evacuated in 1,300 buses, 200 trams and trolleybuses and 180 Underground and Tube trains before continuing on to their destinations in 180 steam trains.

We took ourselves off to Bognor Regis, although my father continued to work in London, but by then access to coastal towns was restricted and most evacuees found themselves experiencing for the first time in their lives the delights or otherwise of a rural existence for which very few were prepared. Children, being adaptable, often took considerable delight in all this, but many did not, either through homesickness or ill treatment by those in whose care they were placed.

Perhaps surprisingly, petrol rationing did not happen quite so quickly but was eventually introduced on 22 September 1939. Fuel supplies to London Transport were reduced by 25%, but, as there was less demand for its services, with many businesses being evacuated and others operating on a much-reduced level, this was not quite as inconvenient as it might have been. Getting on for 1,000 Central Area buses were taken out of service, and some of these were also evacuated, a number serving in the provinces for periods varying from a few weeks to several years. Conversely, once bombing raids began on London, provincial buses were drafted in, although it has been suggested that this was a propaganda move to show solidarity with the capital rather than the result of dire necessity. These buses represented a real mixed bag — some quite modern, many elderly and all very different from the standardised fleet of AECs and Leylands which had been

STL2122, a former Central Area vehicle still in red livery, working from Luton garage. *Ian Allan Library*

built up since 1933. For those who had to maintain this motley collection it must have brought back memories of the 'pirate' fleets absorbed into London Transport seven years earlier. Certainly it is odd that such a mixed bunch should have been sent for when a number of standard (if elderly) London buses were out of service and being held in reserve.

During the war many buses, trams, trolleybuses, coaches and trains were destroyed, although, given the intensity of the Blitz and the later devastation by the V1 'flying bombs' and finally the V2 rockets, perhaps not as many as might be expected. Many more were damaged, patched up and returned to service, often with windows boarded up. Staff and passengers were killed, although (if at all possible) vehicles stopped when the air-raid sirens sounded and shelter was sought. Garages, stations, depots and other buildings were also hit, but services never came to a complete halt; indeed, the staff became adept at performing near-miracles in keeping some sort of service running however devastating the damage of the previous night, for, after the initial days of the Blitz and before the final 'flying bomb' and rocket attacks, most bombing raids took place during the hours of darkness.

In September 1939 London possessed probably the largest municipal fleet of passenger road and rail vehicles in the world; there were 1,316 trams, 1,411 trolley-buses, 5,138 Central Area (red) buses, 604 Country Area (green) buses, 465 coaches and some 3,629 Underground/

Tube carriages. In England, Wales and Scotland there were 90,000 PSVs all told, including taxis, meaning that around one in 10 of the country's public-transport vehicles operated in the London area. The total of cars and light vans in the UK, excluding Northern Ireland, was 2,034,000; in the 1940s the vast majority depended on public transport.

The furthest north the London Passenger Transport Board's vehicles reached was Baldock, terminus of Green Line route K1; eastwards they reached Tilbury and Gravesend, twin towns on opposite banks of the Thames, where several Green Line and Country Area bus routes terminated; in the south they could be found at Horsham, terminus of Green Line K3 and Country buses 414 and 434, whilst to the west it was a tie between West Wycombe and Aylesbury, the former the terminus of the 455A, the latter that of the 301, the 359 and Green Line B and E.

One of my most vivid memories of the 1940s is of sitting at the front — where else? — of the top deck of an Embankment-bound tram and looking down Brixton Hill. From this great height I could see two lines of trams stretching towards the horizon, which was formed by two railway bridges — one high, one low — in front of which yet more trams infiltrated and intersected, accompanied by double-deck buses, some of them six-wheelers.

Michael H. C. Baker
February 2003

• 1 •

The Fleet

THE six-wheel buses in London's fleet at the outbreak of war were AEC Renowns, both double- and single-deck, of the LT class. The oldest dated from 1929 and were due for imminent withdrawal, but the war would prolong their lives by almost a decade. The standard London double-deck bus at the beginning of 1940 was the 56-seat STL-class AEC Regent, the last of which (STL2645) entered service from Alperton garage on 4 September 1939. (It should be explained at this point that within the STL class there were all sorts of variations, the type having originated with the General and Tilling companies in 1932/3; indeed, there would be further STLs, but none which could, strictly speaking, be called standard.) The RT, successor to the STL, was already in existence, but only the prototype was at work, the first of the production batch not entering passenger service until 2 January 1940.

We shall return to the RT — one of the all-time classic British buses — in due course, but let us first consider the STL. There was a time, in the years following this type's withdrawal from passenger service in London in 1954, when it would have been hard to argue that this too was a classic, but of late there has been a re-evaluation of its many qualities. Today the final prewar version is seen as a fine example of the bus builder's art — from the point of view of passengers, drivers and operator as advanced a PSV as any on the road at that time. The superb restoration carried out by the London Bus Preservation Trust at Cobham of STL2377 has reminded those of us who remember the STL the first time round (or revealed to those who don't) what a magnificent vehicle it was. Interestingly it is turned out in the condition in which it appeared after its first overhaul (rather than as when brand-new) and thus exactly as it would have been at the beginning of 1940.

Concurrent with the STL was the STD — the Leyland version of the standard London double-decker. This was based on the Titan TD4 chassis and fitted with a Leyland body heavily disguised to resemble a roofbox STL; in this Leyland had done a pretty good job, although the differences were not hard to spot. There were only 100 STDs, all based at Hendon, but they were to have some influence on the RT and the postwar fleet and were a familiar sight in Central London, working the 113, which terminated at Oxford Circus, and (best known of all) the 13, which continued on to London Bridge station.

A design which might have transformed British double-deck design many years before the Leyland Atlantean did so was the side-engined AEC Q. Four were built in 1934 — two in red livery and two in green. All later worked in the Country Area but were withdrawn on the outbreak of war and never ran again in London. The single-deck version was much more numerous and successful and lasted in some numbers until the 1950s.

An example of the final version of the standard prewar double-decker, the 15STL16, STL 2624, with long radiator, is seen working out of Hanwell garage in postwar days, shortly before the chassis was rebuilt to form the basis of an SRT and the body transferred to one of the STL2014-2188 series. *Alan Cross*

An 'E3' tram and an 'H1' trolleybus meet in Woolwich. *R. Hubble*

Elephant & Castle, one of the busiest traffic intersections in London, is the setting for this prewar view including a 'Bluebird' LT, four early STLs and a long line of trams. *Collectorcard*

Above: Tram route 57 was replaced by trolleybus route 557 (Liverpool Street station–Chingford Mount) some two months before the outbreak of war. Many trams retained open platforms into 1940. Despite its archaic appearance, 'E1' No 566 was built as recently as 1930. When one considers that the ultra-modern 'Feltham' trams were under construction in 1930 one wonders what on earth the LCC was thinking of in perpetuating a design which went back to 1907, at which time many of its competitors were horse-drawn. *Alan Cross*

Above: Tram No 1370 could probably claim to be the only new tram built by London Transport. It was reconstructed in 1933 from the remains of a badly damaged 'E1' car dating from 1910, with a complete new upper deck and new seating throughout. A most handsome car, it is seen with white-painted domed roof before being renumbered 2. *Author's collection*

Right: London Transport made an attempt to upgrade the 'E1' class by rehabilitating 154 of them. Their interiors were certainly an improvement, as this view of restored No 1622, which is in regular service at the National Tramway Museum at Crich, demonstrates. *Author*

A view inside Harrow Weald garage in immediate prewar days. A mechanic is working on the rear of a standard ST. Next to it (believe it or not) is an STL; this was originally a Redline Birch-bodied bus, given a secondhand body dating from 1930. It started out with an open staircase which was later enclosed, but then, remarkably, London Transport rebuilt it with an open staircase once again and route boards instead of roller blinds. On its right is a 5Q5 of 1936, Q142. *London Transport*

The last chance for survival of the London tram beyond the early 1940s, had not the war intervened, was the magnificent 'Feltham'. Here, after transfer to south-side work, one is towed around Charlton Works by a tractor. A turntable is set amongst the cobbles in the foreground. *Author's collection*

Predecessors of the STLs and contemporaries of the six-wheel LTs were shorter-wheelbase AEC Regents of the ST class. There were many versions of both ST and LT, the oldest due for replacement; indeed, the 191 ex-Tilling open-staircase STs were in the course of withdrawal when war broke out.

The standard single-decker was the T-class AEC Regal, although, strictly speaking, no one class can be said to have had a monopoly of the term 'standard' in the late 1930s, in the way that the STL was the standard double-decker. The T also originated with 'the General', many being used on Green Line work, although others came from Thomas Tilling and a whole host from smaller operators. The newest Ts — the handsome 10T10 Green Line coaches — were little more than a year old but had already been superseded by a remarkable Leyland design, the TF. These initials signified

Green Line 9T9 coach T420c about to set off for Watford from Reigate garage. The heavily built-up front end was refined in their much more numerous and highly successful 10T10 successors.
London Country

Above: 10T10 interior. Not really a coach by long-distance standards. *Author*

Right: Now this really is a luxury coach. One of the Private Hire six-wheel LTC Renowns. *London Transport*

Left: Deep in the rural fastness of a winter day in the Surrey Hills, T599 steadily climbs a deep-set lane through the North Downs on its way to Abinger. Introduced in 1938, the 10T10s were the backbone of the Green Line network but worked as Country Area buses too. The outline of the conductor can be seen through the nearside window, a reminder that two-man crews were the norm in the days of half-cab single-deckers. *London Transport*

Above: C60, one of the little 20-seat Leyland Cubs, in suitably bucolic Hertfordshire surroundings. *London Transport*

Top left: One of the production flat-floor-engine Leyland Tigers: Green Line TF16c, based at Romford garage for route X. *London Transport*

Lower left: TF9, the only Private Hire TF to survive the bombing at Bull's Yard, Peckham. *Alan B. Cross*

Tiger Flat, the position of the horizontal engine pointing the way to what would become standard practice in the bus and coach industry in the early 1950s. Despite this the TF class still sported the traditional half-cab layout, thus negating one of the primary advantages of the horizontal, underfloor engine. Most TFs were Green Line coaches, but 12 had elegant Park Royal bodywork and were allocated to the Private Hire fleet; these would have tragically short lives, all but TF9 being destroyed during the Blitz in October 1940.

London Transport inherited a fascinating but impractical variety of small buses operating in both Central and Country areas, and one of its many priorities was to standardise upon a replacement. Leyland had its Cub, introduced in 1931, and a prototype — C1 — was ordered and put in service in October 1934. Its Chiswick-built body was a typically handsome version of current practice, with a strong family likeness to contemporary T and STL classes. The prototype having proved itself, 96 production examples were ordered. This time the bodies were built not by Chiswick but by Short Bros (which firm would soon concentrate on

aircraft production) and Weymann. They were divided between the Central and Country areas.

There were two further variations on the Cub theme. In 1936 eight highly distinctive forward-control buses with 1½-deck Park Royal bodywork, painted blue and yellow with black roofs, were bought for the Inter Station service. This was one of the many services abandoned on the outbreak of war, the buses (C106-13) being loaned to the Entertainments National Service Association (better known as ENSA) for the duration. ENSA's role was to put on shows for the troops and those engaged in war work in factories all over the country, and the Cubs travelled far and wide, conveying concert parties (not always, it must be said, of the highest quality) to places no London bus had ever previously visited.

London Transport was extraordinarily inventive when it came to single-deckers. Following on the revolutionary Qs and TFs, was the CR class of 49 Leyland Cubs with rear-mounted diesel engines. The prototype took up work at the beginning of 1938, whilst the production batch appeared between September 1939 and February 1940. It was an unfortunate time for an experimental design. CR18 was gone within a year, destroyed when a bomb fell on the Bull Yard, Peckham, in October 1940; the same bomb also destroyed all but one of the Private Hire TFs — Hitler must have had a particular down on unusual single-deckers. Mechanically the CRs were far from reliable — a serious shortcoming when the engineering side of London Transport was under desperate pressure. In addition there was little use for buses of such limited capacity in wartime

conditions. Some were never licensed, whilst the remainder had all been put in store by mid-summer 1942. They reappeared after the war, at a time when every single serviceable bus was being pressed into service, but soon disappeared again from the streets of London. CR14 was retained as part of the London Transport collection — the sole survivor of an unfortunate class.

One of the many compromises forced upon London Transport by the outbreak of war was a halt in the programme to convert all tram routes to trolleybus operation. However, despite this, North and East London continued to lose their trams. The West India Docks–Smithfield 77 was replaced by trolleybus 677 in September 1939, the 61 and 63 — linking Aldgate with Leyton and Ilford — gave way to the 661 and 663 in November, and, just before Christmas, Highgate Village lost its tram route 11 when trolleybus 611 took over. Prewar there would be just one more tram-replacement scheme (and the last to involve trolleybuses), the 565, 567 and 665 replacing the Bloomsbury/Smithfield/Aldgate/Holborn Circus–East Ham/West Ham/Poplar/Barking tram routes 65 and 67 in June 1940. Even then, new trolleybuses to full prewar standard continued to be added to the fleet, the last of these — MCW-bodied Leyland 'P1' No 1721 — taking up work from Hammersmith depot in October 1941. It is highly likely that these final 25 vehicles were bought to fill the places of those lost (or liable to be lost) to bombing.

The only variety of the Q class which exploited its potential for having the entrance right at the front was the Park Royal-bodied 5Q5. In theory these could have been one-man-operated, but they were a generation too early for that, hence the conductor smiling for the camera as Q179 of Sidcup garage heads for home, pursued by a Morris post office van. *F. G. Reynolds*

Top left: A pair of 20-seat, one-man-operated Country Area Leyland Cubs, with C22 leading, at Gravesend.

Lower left: One of the BRCW-bodied 4Q4s, Q92, at St Albans. *Ian Allan Library*

Below: The original rear-engined Leyland Cub, CR1, as delivered in July 1938. *London Transport*

· 2 ·

Wartime 'Make Do and Mend'

IN October 1941 the first of the wartime utility buses was shown to the press. This was vastly less well appointed than trolleybus No 1721, neither chassis nor body being up to the standard Londoners had come to expect. Wartime restrictions meant no lining to the upper-deck ceiling, no double panelling below the windows, and brown leathercloth upholstery. The chassis was the Leyland Titan TD7 and was totally unsuitable for Central London. Gear-changing was painfully slow, and drivers hated them. These 11 buses were the prelude to hundreds more utility buses, although there would be no more Leylands until the war was over. They were added to the STD class but were not a patch on their predecessors, the TD4s based at Hendon, which had all sorts of modifications to make them suitable for the demands of a life in Central

Authority and the times decreed that nothing could save the tram from extinction. This is Poplar depot in May 1940, with a group of chassisless 'L3' trolleybuses waiting to enter service. Note the wartime white stripe at the bottom edge of their platforms. *Ian Allan Library*

London. Despite this they spent all their lives based at the most central of all London's garages, Gillingham Street, Victoria, and managed to give 10 years' passenger service before being retired in 1951.

Next to arrive were nine Bristols, in the spring of 1942. Bristol was a make quite unknown in London, but the LPTB was desperate for new buses. They had five-cylinder Gardner engines (hence the designation K5G) and Park Royal bodies more or less identical to those fitted to the STDs. They were much less sophisticated than London's prewar AECs and Leylands, but the mechanics and drivers at Hanwell garage, where they were sent, thought better of them than did the staff at Victoria of their STDs. These Bristols (forming the B class) and the STDs were known as 'unfrozen' vehicles — many of their components were already in stock but the Ministry of Supply had initially ordered that work on them be stopped so that the factories could go over to war work, but it soon became clear that a certain number of new buses would have to be produced each year to make up for war losses and life-expired withdrawals.

Victoria station in immediate prewar days. Amongst the variety of STs, LTs and STLs is a new roofbox STL with gleaming unpainted radiator. *Author's collection*

Metro-Cammell-bodied AEC 'H1' trolleybus No 768 passes tram No 538 on route 3, which succumbed to trolleybuses in July 1938. No 538 is an 'E' class car, predecessor of the 'E1', and was built in 1906. Apart from a single example rebuilt as an 'E1', all the 'Es' had gone by the end of 1938. *London Transport*

The former ST40 in use as a tree-lopper in wartime. Originally a standard LGOC bus, it was taken out of passenger service, possibly as a result of war damage, and given a converted Lewis Omnibus Co body for its new role. *Ian Allan Library*

No 418J, an AEC heavy-emergency breakdown lorry of 1939, used to clear Underground breakdowns. Equipped with a radio, it was on 24-hour standby. *London Transport*

What the LPTB wanted most were AECs, and 34 'unfrozen' Regent chassis duly arrived between the end of 1941 and the autumn of 1942, to be added to the STL class. Chiswick produced a like number of bodies, 20 to lowbridge layout, the designers managing to adapt the standard STL look pretty successfully; internally, however (like the 'unfrozen' STDs), all fell far short of prewar standards. In the event, all 20 lowbridge bodies were mounted on overhauled prewar chassis (as was one of the highbridge ones), which meant that most of the 'unfrozen' chassis received various types of earlier, overhauled bodywork. STL2674/9 each received one of the earliest LGOC STL1-type bodies; they were destined to be the last survivors, and one very nearly got preserved. The highbridge bodies, coded STL17/1, looked very much like the last series of prewar vehicles but internally were to skimpy wartime standards. All went to work in the Country Area and I got to know them well on our local 409 and 411 routes when they were based at Godstone garage. Like the STDs the chassis were built to provincial rather than London specifications but were much better received, being well suited to Country Area work and steep hills, such as that encountered on the climb from Caterham Valley to Caterham-on-the-Hill.

These Leylands, AECs and Bristols represented something of a halfway house — or rather bus — between full prewar standards and the very downmarket full wartime version which came next, by the hundred. But first there arrived 43 trolleybuses which while not exactly 'unfrozen' (overheated?) were certainly unexpected. Intended for Durban and Johannesburg, they never made the long and potentially hazardous journey south but instead took the next-best option and settled in Ilford. Despite having Leyland or AEC chassis and MCW bodywork they were very different from anything seen previously in London (or, indeed, the UK), being

STL2666, one of the 'unfrozen' buses fitted with a highbridge body, working from Godstone garage. Seen at the Swan & Sugar Loaf, South Croydon, it has neither roofbox nor opening windows at the front. *Author's collection*

fitted with such tropical devices as full-drop windows (some of them darkened) and entrances at the front as well as at the rear. Perhaps most significantly they were 8ft wide, which caused the Metropolitan Police a sharp intake of breath, nothing wider than 7ft 6in having been permitted hitherto. Special dispensation was duly granted, and the trolleys (Classes SA1, SA2 and SA3) settled down to uneventful lives in the Ilford and Barking areas.

Completing half-finished prewar vehicles or diverting those intended for export was no long-term answer to the need for new buses, so the Government authorised a resumption of production, albeit strictly controlled.

No 1731, one of the trolleybuses intended for Durban, South Africa, but delivered to London Transport in 1941, which spent its career working in the Ilford area. *Author's collection*

Bedford supplied single-deckers — little single-deck, normal-control OWBs — but these were of no interest to London. The plan was that both Leyland and Guy should produce double-deck chassis, but in the event Leyland concentrated on other war work, so that double-deck bus chassis were available only from Guy. Neither the LGOC nor the LPTB had favoured this make, but now there was no choice, and between August 1942 and March 1946 no fewer than 435 Guy Arabs entered London service. Later Daimler was also permitted to produce buses, and a total of 281 joined the LPTB fleet, the first arriving in April 1944, the last in November 1946. Most of the Daimlers were fitted with AEC engines, which alone would have made them more welcome; drivers also found them to be more responsive than the Guys.

Passengers, not surprisingly, cared little about chassis variation. The comfort and general appointments of the interiors was their chief concern, and they were to be sadly disappointed. A variety of manufacturers — many, such as Park Royal and Weymann, well known to London, others, like Northern Counties and Massey, less so — supplied bodies, but unseasoned timber and strict instructions to cut down on what were now considered luxuries (but had in the 1930s been thought of as essential) produced a very basic, rather primitive vehicle. There were few opening windows, and rock bottom was reached when some were delivered with wooden seats. However, contrasts with standard STs, LTs and STLs were not always as marked as they might have been, for maintenance standards inevitably dropped, overhauls were long overdue, windows broken

D3 was one of the first batch of wartime Daimlers; a Duple-bodied lowbridge example fitted originally with wooden seats, it was delivered to Merton garage in May 1944. It is seen waiting at a favourite haunt of the Daimlers, the forecourt of the Northern Line station at Morden. *Alan Cross*

Having just deposited a mother and child, G145, a Park Royal-bodied Guy delivered in June 1945, waits amongst the wide open spaces of Wembley for an elderly 8hp delivery van to move out of its way. *F. G. Reynolds*

by bomb blasts were boarded up, paintwork deteriorated, interior and exterior lighting was reduced, and the whole fleet became shabbier and shabbier.

One surprising aspect of the wartime world of 'making do and mend' (with ever-more-stretched engineers trying to keep buses, trams and trolleybuses on the road, despite the severe shortage of materials and spare parts) was the continued advertisement of manufacturers' products. Not only, of course, does advertising cost money but there was so little choice that one would not have thought it worthwhile. Yet, right through the war, every edition of the weekly *Passenger Transport Journal* contains slogans such as 'If trolley 'buses had a flying start they would be finished in TITANINE, the world's premier aeroplane finish', complete with a jolly picture of a pair of wings protruding from 'D2' Leyland No 456 as it skims above Wandsworth on its way to 'near Willesden Junction'. In another advertisement STL934 negotiates a snow-covered street above the slogan headed 'Dirty Work at the Cross Roads' and

Right: Heavily boarded-up STL1456 on an emergency service. *Alan Cross collection*

Below: The austere lower-deck interior of a wartime double-decker, in this instance a Guy dating from 1943. Amongst the wartime features are the low-back wooden seats, the netting over the windows (of which there's only one opening one on each side) and the heavy shades over the lamps. *London Transport*

Britain's Standard War-Time Buses

Simplified Design to Meet Present Conditions

AT the works of a well-known coachbuilding concern recently we were afforded the opportunity of inspecting the first double-deck bus produced under a war-time programme to meet urgent passenger transport requirements. This vehicle, which has a seating capacity of 56, is the forerunner of many others to be built under a comprehensive scheme at numerous coachbuilding works in various parts of the country. Simplification in design and specification, along with the standardisation of fittings, will facilitate ease of

facturers' works. It was only on closer inspection that the deletion of some of the customary frills and trimmings became apparent. It must not be thought that the new standard war-time product is lacking in comfort. In fact, to the untrained eye, it would indeed be difficult to distinguish the war-time model from the peace-time prototype. Comfort in seating has not been sacrificed, but the luxuries of the usual plenitude of drop windows, heaters, decorative mouldings, have been curtailed so as to eliminate present unnecessary fixtures and fittings.

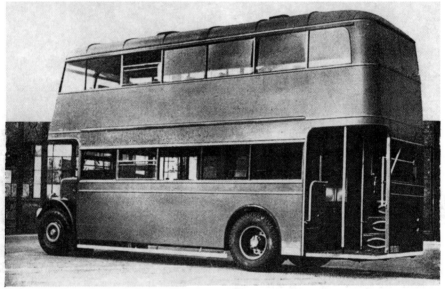

Side view of the new standard war-time double-deck bus.

production and provide considerable economies in man hours and in the use of essential materials.

These vehicles are being built to the instructions of the Ministry of Supply and on completion they will be issued through the Ministry of War Transport to operator undertakings whose war-time requirements are most urgent. The design and specification are the work of a joint committee consisting of technical representatives of the National Federation of Vehicle Trades and the Joint Passenger Transport Operators organisation.

At first sight there appeared to be little difference in the appearance of the war-time bus from that of the normal vehicle. True, the drab grey war-time garb seemed somewhat unfamiliar when compared with the bright red, green or other such livery usually associated with a new vehicle ready to be driven away into service from the manu-

In general the bodywork complies with the current regulations of the Ministry of Transport and the seating is arranged to accommodate 26 in the lower saloon and 30 in the upper saloon. In the case of low-bridge types of vehicles, of which a number are being built for use in certain localities, a slight modification of the seating arrangements has been necessary, although 55 persons are carried—28 in the lower saloon and 27 on the upper deck.

The specification calls for body framing to be of oak, ash, mahogany or teak, with the exception of longitudinal rails, which may be of pitch pine. The framing is strengthened where necessary with flitches and gussets of steel in accordance with standard practice.

The top and bottom deck hoopsticks are of selected ash, strengthened with flitches or carlines

Left: A page from the *Passenger Transport Journal* of 14 November 1941, depicting an STD-type Leyland Titan TD7 before painting into London Transport livery. *Passenger Transport Journal*

Right: Even though it was now impossible to buy a new AEC bus, this advert, depicting a 9T9, appeared in the *Passenger Transport Journal* of 19 December 1941. *Passenger Transport Journal*

IT'S WORTH REMEMBERING that although the Road to Victory is long and hard, it's getting shorter every day. KEEP IT UP!

BUILDERS OF LONDON'S BUSES

Published by the Proprietors, H. F. Maynard, Ltd., Avenue Chambers, Southampton Row, London, W.C.1, Temporary address, Stratton, Biggleswade, Bedfordshire, and Printed by Charles Elphick, at Biggleswade, Bedfordshire, England.

emphasising the 'smooth power' of Westinghouse brakes, whilst on the same theme a group of vehicles on Westminster Bridge (including a couple of STLs, an 'E1' tram, a Morris 8 and a Humber Snipe) are supposed to persuade us of the 'greater stopping power and safer control' of Ferodo brake linings. Nobels & Hoare of Stamford Street, SE1, modestly claimed that Vincomel, the synthetic enamel was 'especially suitable for all types of new work'. However, in June 1941 we are assured that Cerrux synthetic finishes were 'the final word in finishes', and to prove it we are shown a picture of centre-entrance 'Feltham' No 331 (upon which we may still happily ride at the National Tramway Museum at Crich); I wonder if Cerrux realised that No 331 had migrated to Sunderland several years earlier?

One of the least-explicable advertisements was one placed by Leyland. A splendid full-page picture of STD33 and an Austin taxi negotiating Trafalgar Square, clearly taken before the war, appears over the slogan 'Leylands last longer', which may well have been true but was meaningless in the spring of 1941, when this great manufacturer's entire output was devoted to the war effort. No less odd is the advertisement which Leyland's great rival, AEC, published as the war was ending, in the 1945 *Passenger Transport Journal Year Book*, showing a line of vehicles headed by two six-wheel double-deckers — a Leicester Renown and a Q! Whatever AEC's production plans for the postwar years, I've never heard anyone suggest that either the Q or the Renown would feature!

· 3 ·

Coping with War

DESPITE fears of immediate devastation in September 1939, the first air raids were a long time coming. It was not until 16 August 1940 that any damage was suffered by London Transport, when trolleybus wires were brought down by a bomb in New Malden; services were restored in just over four hours. That is the official story, although there is more than a possibility that LT260 was actually the first London Transport vehicle to suffer war damage, being caught up in a raid on Croydon Aerodrome in June 1940. Tram and trolleybus services were obviously prone to more dislocation than were motor-bus routes, which could be diverted, but the motor bus used precious petrol and diesel. The Luftwaffe initially attacked RAF aerodromes and other military installations, chiefly on the South Coast, but Hitler was so enraged by a token RAF raid on Berlin that he ordered his air force to turn its attention to London. Strategically this was a mistake, for it took the pressure off Fighter Command, which was at full stretch defending its own bases, but it meant that London — and Londoners — began to suffer fearfully.

Inevitably the area around the docks in the East End bore the brunt of the bombing, both because the raiders could easily follow the Thames as they came in over the estuary between Southend and the Kent Coast and because of its strategic importance. It was thus somewhat ironic that some of the first actual damage to

LPTB property should be way over in the western suburbs, but once August had given way to September and the Battle of Britain was at its height, the bombing reached its terrifying intensity, and on 7 September 1940 a raid began around teatime and continued through to dawn the next day. Centred on the docks, the East End and the City, it consisted of incendiary bombs which totally overwhelmed the fire services. No London Transport vehicle was actually destroyed on 7/8 September, but the disruption to services was enormous, and the trolleybus network (in particular) suffered, both north and south of the river. Much of this, the routes 565, 567 and 665 along the Commercial Road and West India Dock Road had only just been introduced, in June, replacing the last of the East London trams north of the river. There were deaths and many injuries to staff and passengers, although when an raid was expected — and Britain's lead in perfecting radar gave vital minutes to prepare — buses, trams and trolleys usually stopped and passengers and crews hurried to the nearest shelters whenever possible.

It is worth quoting in some detail an article in the 14 April 1941 issue of the *Passenger Transport Journal*:

'Records hitherto considered impossible have been made by London Transport's engineers and the gangs of specially trained men who are kept ready day and night to repair interruptions caused by bombing to

An 'E3' tram emerges from the north end of Kingsway Subway and prepares to head into what has now (by 1940) become the trolleybus stronghold of North London. *B. Y. Williams*

London's trolleybus routes, which cover about 250 miles of roads. There is no waiting for instructions. The men are quickly on the spot, and their training enables them to do immediately whatever may be necessary to restore the through running of the services. Cables may be strung along trees in the street or over bushes in private front gardens, or complicated engineering work may have to be undertaken. Two examples of this work may be given.

'At a late hour one night four bombs fell on a road in North London, blowing down a number of bays of trolleybus wires and littering the road with debris. A gang was on the spot at midnight and as usual set to work immediately, although the "alert" was still on and bombs were still dropping. Whilst the linesmen replaced the wires, other men cleared the road of debris so that the first trolleybus ran through next morning at the normal time, 5.00 a.m. This is not an isolated incident. It is typical of the speed with which repairs are effected in all similar cases.

'On another night a bomb fell on a road in South London and left a wide crater entirely blocking the road to vehicular traffic. Working through the darkness, with bombs still falling, the repairmen made temporary arrangements by which trolleybuses could be run to either side of the crater, whence passengers could walk around the gap. At daylight it was decided, in consultation with the police and the

Watched by a fascinated crowd of onlookers, 'E1' No 1545, with badly damaged upper deck, is pushed home for rehabilitation. *Author's collection*

local authority, not to wait for the crater to be filled in but to restore through running of the services by erecting a wholly new system of overhead wires more than a quarter of a mile long so that the trolleybuses could be diverted along two nearby roads which had never had trolleybuses before.

'One obstacle to rapid completion of the job was the absence of any large buildings to which to attach the "span-wires" so that new poles had to be erected over the whole section. Additional difficulties were the narrowness of the roadways and six sharp corners. Trolleybuses could not pass one another at certain points and over a portion of the route two roads had to be used and one-way working instituted. Because of the presence of service mains, which abound near dwelling houses, all holes for the trolley poles had to be drilled by hand. A delayed-action bomb in one of the roads also set back the work a little.

'Despite these difficulties the detour of 500 yards had been "planted" with 43 poles, each six feet deep in the ground, complete with their overhead within a few days of the bombing. Even the white rings which distinguish the poles during the blackout had been painted upon them.'

Right: Following a raid on the Strand, LT238 is prepared for towing-away on the morning after — 10 October 1940. *P. J. Marshall*

Far right: A sturdy-looking breakdown tender waits for the call inside Riverside garage, Hammersmith, in 1948. No 219U was originally an LS six-wheel double-decker, predecessor of the LT, and was converted for this role in 1936. *M. Dryhurst collection*

The casual reference to the unexploded bomb 'setting back the work a little' speaks volumes for the wartime spirit. Which is not to say that people were not terrified and liable to panic in a bombing raid. At the height of the Blitz on the Docks, East Enders would clamber onto buses and trolleys sometimes in appalling states of shock and disarray, heading for the relative safety of further west, to be confronted by residents of the West End and beyond who refused to sit with them; some even complained to the authorities about their state.

South of the river, London's trams faced equal dangers. The 30 May 1941 issue of *Passenger Transport Journal* records the experiences of one driver. After explaining that the all-night trams had never ceased running since the war began, despite their routes' lying through some of the worst-blitzed areas (albeit having been changed or shortened on occasion), the account continues:

Left: Wartime in the East End. Workers at Silvertown board an unidentified trolleybus whilst, in the background, another (No 795A, which had been rebodied after being damaged in the Blitz) is overtaken by an impressive-looking Leyland lorry. *London Transport*

Right: Old Kent Road garage in September 1940. Originally a tram depot, it was converted for bus use as early as 1907. In this picture it houses a collection of LT double deckers, a Q single decker and an AEC lorry. The roof had to be raised when RTs replaced the LTs in 1948, the former being slightly taller. The garage closed in November 1958. *Author's collection*

'One of the drivers is Mr. Sidney Herbert Ball, of Tooting, who has been working on trams, first as a conductor and then as a driver, for 34 years. He is now aged 56, but he looks much younger. Apart from his nights off, he has driven his tram out of the Streatham Depot every night since the war began, bombs or no bombs. In the dark winter months he frequently had to walk for 45 to 50 minutes from his home to his depot, which he leaves, according to the "duty" he is on, at midnight, 12.30 or 1 a.m. His tram makes four figure-of-eight journeys between Telford Avenue and Victoria Embankment.

'Mr. Ball was on trams — then as an L.C.C. man — throughout the last war. He enjoys his work and says that it takes more than Hitler's bombs to frighten him. Bombs have fallen close to his tram on many occasions and several times he has helped to save buildings by putting out incendiary bombs. One night he saw an incendiary bomb roll under the outer door of a large building. There was just space under the door to admit the bomb, but not space for him to crawl under. He and some passengers tried to batter down the door without success and soon the building was blazing. Much worse than the bombs is the black-out. It is difficult to judge distances and in the darkness his eyes play odd tricks. Mr. Ball has often pulled up his tram, believing that a vehicle had stopped on the track, only to find what he thought was a red rear lamp was a glowing cigarette end, sticking upon the road.

'Mr. Ball takes an interest in his passengers and they take an interest in him. Before the war they were a colourful and often gay crowd — cabaret girls, dance girls, music hall performers, newspapermen, waiters, market workers and cleaners. Now that entertainments end much earlier, Mr. Ball's passengers are mostly newspapermen and soldiers on leave who have stayed in the West End as late as

possible. Mr. Ball says that during a "rough" night passengers frequently come to his cab, shake him by the hand and thank him for having got them home. This pleases Mr. Ball, who is known to many of his passengers by his Christian name of Sid. He is not always able to run as strictly to timetable as in peacetime, but he still tries to keep passengers waiting in the blacked-out and often dangerous streets as little as possible and he never leaves anyone behind.

'Mr. Ball has no nerves. He feels happier and safer in his large, Feltham-type tramcar than in a house or in the street. His passengers too, seem to be content in the car, but he has one interesting and perhaps surprising comment to make — elderly people withstand bombing much better than do young people. He has yet to see an elderly person, man or woman, give the slightest sign of being frightened.'

The 'Felthams' certainly were superb vehicles — and very strong — but were surely not impervious to a German bomb. Several were damaged during the war, although only two (Nos 2109 and 2113) so badly that they could not be repaired.

Certain old habits died hard in wartime. Passengers still managed to leave vast amounts of property behind. Apart from the usual collection of umbrellas, bags and all manner of personal belongings, in just one week in September 1940, no fewer than 3,000 gas masks and steel helmets were left on the Board's vehicles.

Bombs were hardly a laughing matter, but inevitably some of the newspaper accounts managed to find a lighter side to Blitz stories. The *South London Press*, which always devoted a whole page of its scarce newsprint to the local courts, noted that James Arthur Bastow (37), a builder from Wandsworth, was 'causing a fuss' in a pub one Saturday evening, as a result of which a policeman was called. Bastow happens to have had in his possession an unexploded incendiary bomb — we are not told why — and proceeded to try to hit the police constable with it. The next morning the magistrate enquired of Bastow if he thought hitting a policeman 'was the thing to do with a bomb' and, without waiting for an answer, fined him 10s.

Ten shillings (50p) was the value of the old-age pension in 1940. Around this time fares, which had remained unchanged for years, were raised. An elderly man boarded a bus at Camberwell Green and asked the conductor for a penny fare, explaining he was going 'to the Town Hall for me pension'. On being told that the fare was now a penny-ha'penny he replied: 'That's all right, son, you can't help it. Makes a difference, though, when you're on ten bob a week and can't walk anywhere.'

One of the most extraordinary statistics to emerge during the Blitz was the rise in the number of road deaths directly attributable to the blackout, there being many more accidents during the hours of darkness than there had been in peacetime. Mostly they involved pedestrians colliding with vehicles. Practically every issue of the London local papers during the Blitz notes deaths or serious injuries, often involving buses, trolleys or trams. Sometimes, in the almost pitch dark, people followed the tram lines in order to find their way, but this could lead to disaster. On 29 June 1940 a tram driver, Sydney Goodall, was summoned before the local magistrates following a fatal accident in Balham. He described how he had been driving at no more than 8-9mph at 11.30pm when 'a man's face loomed out of the darkness'. He slammed on the brakes with such force that his conductor was sent flying down the length of the car, but could not avoid the man, who was found lying in the road and died next day. A verdict of accidental death was recorded.

When an air raid was expected, drivers were supposed to stop their vehicles beside the nearest shelter and, before leaving, extinguish all lights, except those at the front and rear. These were fitted with shades and could

Piccadilly Circus at the height of the war. Eros has flown from his plinth, joining thousands of others in being evacuated from the capital. Private cars, no doubt all engaged on essential war work, have not entirely disappeared as an LT and four STLs — one with considerably more wood than glass in its windows — make their dignified way into or out of Regent Street.
Ian Allan Library

be very difficult to see. Another unfortunate tram driver summoned before magistrates was a Camberwell man. His car 'crashed into the rear of a stationary tram outside Lewisham Hospital at 11.40 on the night of July 28, and drove it forward … about 40 yards. Twenty-five persons were injured, including Driver Brewer, who was taken to hospital.' One passenger described how he jumped from the platform and 'landed on his hands and knees, covered with broken glass'. The conductor of the tram in front, having been told there was a 'red' air-raid warning, had turned off his interior lights but claimed he had left his platform lights on.

Mr Brewer said he had seen nothing and, despite being backed up by a passenger, was found guilty and fined 3s (15p), plus 17s 10d (89p) costs.

On the evening of 27 September 1940 a Poplar woman, Mrs Elizabeth Beadle, was killed by a trolleybus in the East India Dock Road whilst out shopping during an air raid. The *Hackney Gazette* of Wednesday 13 November 1940 recorded the death of a Shoreditch man who, crossing the road, was seen to 'throw up his hands and suddenly disappear under the bus, which stopped immediately … the sirens had sounded and there was gunfire overhead.' The driver had served 31 years, had a clean licence and held the

'L3' trolleybus at King's Cross. This was delivered from Metro-Cammell with (most unusually) sliding ventilators, on 3 May 1940, the explanation probably being that wartime shortages precluded the use of the usual half-drops. No 1527 could easily be mistaken for one of the war-damaged rebuilds, which also had this type of window. *Author*

'B1' trolleybus of Carshalton depot loads up by Reeves Corner, West Croydon, on its way from Crystal Palace to Sutton on a winter's day in 1940. In the distance a Country Area STL, still with a complete route display, approaches behind what looks like one of the very last large prewar Morris saloons.
John B. Gent collection

Two roofbox STLs at Aldgate bus station in the early days of the war: Green Line STL2612, one of the final 1939 batch with long radiator and in two-tone green livery, alongside slightly older red STL2321 of 1937 (and identical to the preserved STL2377). *Author's collection*

Safety First silver medal and seven bars. 'The night of the accident was one of the darkest for some time. He had slowed down to four or five miles an hour on approaching a request stop and heard someone shout "Stop!" He applied the brakes and pulled up in a couple of yards. He found the deceased underneath the bus.' The driver was exonerated of all blame for what must have been an appalling experience, and the Deputy Coroner 'paid a tribute to 'bus drivers, remarking that it was amazing that they were involved in so few accidents during the black-out period'.

So serious was the situation regarding the carnage on the roads that the *Hackney Gazette* was driven to deal with it in an editorial in December 1940 under the heading 'Vehicles as deadly as Bombs'. It is worth quoting.

'While most people shelter from bombs, many of them continue to court danger and death on the roads to an alarming degree. It is one of the ironies of wartime existence for which there seems to be no sufficient explanation. Figures show that 19,545 civilians have been killed as the result of bombing since the Germans developed their air offensive on Britain. These compare with a total of 11,434 deaths on the roads during the fifteen months of war — an increase of no fewer than 3,141, or nearly 40 per cent., on the corresponding period immediately preceding the fateful September of last year ... As might be expected, most of the accidents occur in the hours of darkness; but a disturbing fact is that the increase is now relatively higher during daylight. Possibly the hurry and impetuosity engendered by war

conditions, as well as the larger amount of strain to which people are subjected, are mainly responsible for the rise.' The article concludes with two particularly thought-provoking observations. 'Motorists ... may allege that the more rigid limitation of vehicle lighting accentuates risks by restricting visibility and deceiving pedestrians by giving them a false idea of distance or perspective. Some of the latter may even fail to remember that Belisha crossings [named after Hore Belisha, the Government minister responsible for their introduction at the end of the 1930s] are practically valueless, from the point of view of security, in the black-out.'

Various measures were brought in to try to reduce the terrible death toll. New platform lamps, 'softly flood-lighting boarding platforms', were being fitted to buses at the rate of 1,000 a week by the end of September 1940. Earlier in the year the *Passenger Transport Journal* had noted that the Metropolitan Police was complaining that passengers were interfering with the original lampshades, fitted on the outbreak of war, in an effort to obtain more light, and that 20,000 improved ones were now on order. As people grew more used to wartime conditions the numbers of injured and killed on the roads came down, but it remained a problem throughout the war years.

More Tales from the Blitz

In his book *The Wheels used to Talk to Us*, Stan Collins describes an extraordinary night's adventure with a 'Feltham' during the Blitz. One suspects that the account in the previous chapter, being put out officially, was designed to boost morale, for it is difficult to believe that 'Mr. Ball has no nerves', unless he was completely lacking in imagination, but Stan Collins' account rings absolutely true, with nothing left out.

Stan has charge of a No 8, from Victoria to Tooting. Just beyond Vauxhall he is held up by debris from a bomb. 'Just at that moment another bomb fell in Higgs & Hill and the Sunnybank Laundry caught fire. I had the breeze up, I don't mind telling you. "Come on," I said to Alf [Mole, his conductor], "if he sees those fires he'll come back and bomb the hell out of us."' Stan takes a detour towards Nine Elms and is then held up by three trams abandoned by their passengers and drivers who had gone down the shelter under the Southern Railway Club ... 'So I took the hand-brakes off them all, told Alf to stand on the back of the front tram where I could see him, and pushed them all round into

Wandsworth Road. Alf put the hand-brake on the back car as hard as he could — I checked it after, because he was only a Conductor — but there was no chance of the tram running back. Then Alf pulled the points over and we turned into Nine Elms Lane.

'Just past the Dogs' Home there's a railway bridge and I thought, "Oh hell, we're never going to get under there." You see the Feltham was a little bit higher than a Standard, and it had a big base on its trolleys. Very slowly we eased underneath and I could hear the base of the trolleys scraping the bridge, but we cleared that and carried on up past the Latchmere to the Prince's Head.'

Further on, Stan encounters a regulator (inspector) who tells him: '"Felthams have never been up this road yet," ... and I told him that there was one had come up here now and what was he going to do about it? ... I wasn't staying out there all night, not with him dropping them like that. I wanted to get back to Telford.'

After a few more choice exchanges, off he goes. 'I was a bit worried about the bridge at Clapham Junction but I knew trolleybuses went under there, so I thought we'd be alright, and we were.'

Another inspector, 'very ighty-flighty and cocky', tells him to go back because he'd never get his 40ft-long 'Feltham' around the curve into Cedars Road. 'So I took it very steady, I'd got the wind up, little butterflies in my

Three 'K'-class trolleybuses from Stamford Hill amidst the warehouses of the London Docks at the terminus of the 647, a route which replaced tram 47 in February 1939. *Author*

Above: Aldgate East. In the foreground is a trolleybus approaching the Aldgate terminus of the 661; this replaced the Bow trams which had worked route 61 until 5 November 1939. *London Transport*

Below: Weymann-bodied AEC 'J2' trolleybus No 976 turns in front of Smithfield meat market. *London Transport*

stomach, and very gently we came round the curve. I'm leaning out of the near-side cab window working the controller with my right hand and the kerb's coming nearer and nearer as the front swings round … and as I came round the pilot gate just touched the kerb and then we were on the straight.'

Stan's progress comes to a halt at Clapham, where he finds himself behind a line of 10 stationary trams. 'Anyway we walked along this line of trams but couldn't see any Drivers or Conductors until we came to the café at the Plough which was open all night. By then it was getting on for two o'clock and we stuck there until the all-clear went about five that morning, and God above knows where the Drivers turned up from, but they all came up and away went the trams.'

Eventually Stan arrives back at the depot, to be told by the Depot Inspector that "You'll be on the carpet in the morning," for taking a 'Feltham' where no 'Feltham' had ever been before. In fact, when he eventually does meet the Superintendent — 'nice old fellow, Bill Witty' — 'he congratulated me, wanted to know how I'd done it.'

One of the obvious places to shelter from the nightly air raids was down in the Tube, where one might be 60ft below ground and pretty safe from any bomb. The first such occasion seems to have been at Liverpool Street on 8 September 1940, when a large crowd pushed past LT officials and a handful of troops trying to prevent access, and found shelter on the Central Line platforms. Eventually tunnels built for the as yet unfinished extension were converted into shelters with capacity for 10,000. The *South London Press* of 20 September 1940 recorded that 'South Londoners, abandoning public overground and ground level shelters, are going underground every night in Tube stations causing the

Above: A Matilda tank on its way to 'somewhere in England' — presumably a publicity stunt, as tanks travelling any distance would be carried on special low-loaders. It is negotiating Marble Arch in the company of STL1199 of 1935 and an earlier 60-seat London General 2STL1 type. The date is 19 May 1940. *London Transport*

Left: Trolleybus No 1681, an all-Leyland 'K3', one of the last prewar-design trolleybuses. Delivered in the autumn of 1940, it is seen late in life in Holborn while working from Edmonton depot. *Author*

biggest crushes London Transport staff have ever known … public shelters are almost deserted and early every evening queues of families with bedding and food stand in line four or five deep outside. Police have had to guard the doors since crowds have tried to rush the barriers as the sirens sounded, pushing back passengers trying to emerge. "Women and children only," said the station foreman, knowing the little space available.'

A week later a reporter investigated the situation at the Elephant & Castle. 'It took me a quarter of an hour to get from the station entrance to the platform. Even in the darkened booking hall I stumbled over huddled bodies … going down the stairs I saw mothers feeding infants at the breast. Little boys and girls lay across their parents' bodies because there was no room on the winding stairs … Hundreds of men and women were partially undressed, while small boys and girls slumbered in the foetid atmosphere, absolutely naked. On every jutting beam and spike hung coats, waistcoats, shoes and shopping bags. On the platform, when a train came in, it had to be stopped in the tunnel while police and porters went along pushing in the feet and arms which overhung the line … On the train I sat opposite a pilot on leave. He looked dumbly at that amazing platform. "It's the same all the way along," was all he said.'

For a visual impression of this extraordinary period in London life, head along a few hundred yards westwards from Elephant & Castle station to the Imperial War Museum, where the drawings Henry Moore was commissioned to make down in the shelters are on display.

Ellen Wilkinson, Parliamentary Secretary to the Ministry of Home Security, describing 'some of her shelter problems', said there were large houses in Mayfair — 'whole strings of them in fact' — where people could be billeted, but they could not be persuaded to go from the Isle of Dogs to live in Eaton Square. One woman said to her: "Well, miss, whatever would I do with a flat in Eaton Square? Where do you think I should do my shopping — Harrods?"

In Southwark, local residents complained that 'foreigners' from outside the borough were moving in on their territory. 'Some evenings these treks begin as early as 5 o'clock when women arrive with huge suitcases, large shopping bags, parcels of food, milk and mineral waters.' The Mayor of Camberwell said that 'There is a tendency to stake out claims in

the shelters and regard spaces as private preserves. Because of this I have had to issue an order to wardens in charge of the bigger public shelters that no persons shall be allowed to occupy more space than one person should occupy if that space is needed by another member of the public.' Across the river, at Stoke Newington, a woman appeared in court on just such a charge. A policeman said he was on duty at Turnpike Lane station where some 1,500 people were sheltering when he was called to a disturbance. A woman had tried to reserve an extra place amongst those who had settled down for the night. Her defence was that 'because she was a Jewess some of the people did not want her there and they started pushing her and her things about'. She was fined 20s (£1) plus 8s (40p) costs.

Even in a Tube station safety was not guaranteed, and direct hits on Bank, Balham and Trafalgar Square stations caused many casualties: 56 died and 69 were injured at Bank on 11 January 1941, 68 died at Balham on 14 October 1940, and seven were killed by an avalanche of wet earth after a bomb exploded at the head of an escalator at Trafalgar Square on 12 October 1940.

The worst incident took place at Bethnal Green Central Line tube station on the evening of 3 March 1943 and, ironically, was not caused directly by enemy action but by panic resulting from what people thought was a falling bomb. The Army was testing a new anti-aircraft defence system in Victoria Park, $1/4$ mile from the station, and its detonation resulted in a huge bang which people not surprisingly interpreted as an air raid. I can recall vividly just how enormous such an explosion sounded, even at a distance of a mile or more. Apparently security considerations prevented people knowing what the Army was up to.

There was a rush for the perceived safety of the Underground station. It had been raining, the steps leading down were slippery, a woman fell, more rockets were fired, more people fell, those in the rear, unaware

STL2250, built in 1938 with a standard roofbox body, seen with a wartime lowbridge body. It is working the 410 from Godstone garage. *Phil Picken*

of what was happening at the front, pushed, and the resulting horror may be imagined. On the dimly lit steps, bodies piled upon bodies, and within a horrifyingly short time 27 men, 84 women and 62 children were dead. Alfred Morris, aged 13, told how his aunt was the last to be pulled out alive. 'She was trapped against a wall. I remember she was wearing a heavy coat, and they grabbed hold of her shoulders and pulled her free, and she left her coat and shoes behind. She was black and blue all over.' It was estimated that all the victims died — of asphyxiation — within 10-17 seconds.

Inevitably, given wartime secrecy, the event was kept out of the media as far as possible. It was only in 1993 that a small commemorative plaque was unveiled at the station.

Much easier to penetrate were the Underground stations and the surface Tube stations out in the suburbs. The worst such incident occurred at Bounds Green on the Piccadilly Line, where a bomb demolished some houses which collapsed onto the platforms, killing 19 passengers, including 16 Belgian refugees; 52 people were injured. At the newly rebuilt Sloane Square a Circle Line train was hit, causing 79 injuries on 12 November 1940.

For a while as a child I refused to travel on either the Underground or the Tube — perhaps from fear of what might happen, although I wasn't particularly worried about going down our Anderson shelter in the back garden. Later, when I had summoned up sufficient courage to travel underground, I never passed through Sloane Square on our way to visit the South Kensington museums without a shiver of fear as we entered it and a distinct sense of relief as our train pulled out unscathed. At that time many of the elderly Circle trains were not

Evacuating St Thomas's Hospital, Lambeth, at the beginning of the war and carrying a stretcher case into a Green Line 10T10 based at Battersea and converted to an ambulance. *South London Press*

fitted with automatic doors, and I can recall watching with a mixture of fascination and horror as the door opposite us slowly slid open as we rattled through the darkness. There were literally hundreds of other air raids all over the Underground and Tube systems which caused varying amounts of damage.

After a while the authorities realised they would have to make a virtue out of necessity: some sort of order was brought, shelter marshals were appointed, disused stations were reopened and by the end of 1940 it was said that there was accommodation for everyone. By the beginning of 1941 79 medical aid posts were operating, mostly on the platforms. A post contained an isolation bay with five bunks for the temporary accommodation of any infectious diseases, supply of water, electric heating for sterilising instruments, cupboards for surgical instruments and dressings, and bunks for the nurses. A professional nurse was in charge of each station, assisted by auxiliary Red Cross and St John Ambulance nurses, and a medical officer visited each station every night. Eight deep-level shelters were built adjacent to Tube stations, usually beneath them. Work began at the end of November 1940, but none was completed until 1942, by which time the need for them had diminished. All are still there, having served a variety of purposes (intended or otherwise) over the years, including, inevitably, settings for films and TV dramas, not least an episode of *Doctor Who*. One of the more esoteric uses saw Holborn involved in a study of

Right: RT84 in almost-new condition working from Putney Bridge garage in June 1940. *Alan Cross*

Below:
A London Transport bravery medal. *Ian Allan Library*

cosmic rays. To quote the obituary of the physicist John Barton, who led the experiments, 'The laboratory rooms were reached through a service door on one of the Piccadilly Line platforms. They were linked by an extremely narrow corridor, only wide enough for a single person, running along the edge of what had once been the platform. It was a dry and dusty environment and there were occasional problems caused by rodents chewing cables, but it was nonetheless an extraordinarily convenient site to work.'

Large numbers of LT staff joined the Forces, and by the end of 1940 no fewer than 12,167 were in uniform. By this time 72 had died on active service, but this figure was rather less than the 116 who had been killed whilst carrying out their duties with London Transport in the same period — which gives one some indication of just how much in the front line London and its population were during the Blitz.

Frank Pick, who, along with Lord Ashfield, had shaped London Transport into the magnificent undertaking it had become by September 1939, died suddenly in November 1941 at the age of 62, having retired a little earlier as Vice Chairman of the London Passenger Transport Board.

LONDON TRANSPORT

ALFRED ERNEST SHARMAN
1 NOVEMBER 1940
FOR BRAVERY AND DEVOTION TO DUTY

A solicitor by profession, he was one of those rare men who showed abilities far beyond that for which he was trained and, as his obituary in the *Passenger Transport Journal* noted, 'Mr. Pick was a great transport man and he was at the same time a great scholar. His activities ranged over a wide field. In art circles he was recognised as an expert and connoisseur: he had advanced views on all the problems connected with town planning and he was Chairman of the Council for Art and Industry of the Board of Trade. He was a man of immense intellectual power, and the many papers he wrote for the societies with which he was connected not only showed him as master of his subjects but able to express himself in terms of great lucidity and much literary charm. His team work with Lord Ashfield was one of the great factors in building up the LPTB. Each was the complement of the other, and history will record their partnership as one which had the most beneficent results in evolving from the chaotic traffic conditions which followed the conclusion of the last war the ordered system of transport which, although even now in many respects incomplete, makes traffic conditions in London the envy of most capital cities of the world.'

• 5 •

In the Depths of War

NOT everyone pulled together during the war: there were always those who saw their opportunity in the blackout and shortages. May Cooke, a lady conductor based at Bromley garage, worked the 47 a route which passed through some of the most heavily bombed areas of East London on both sides of the river. 'I found during the late turns that people took advantage of the black-out by giving me farthings instead of sixpences for their fares, and of course I was well out of pocket. Eventually, many clippies bought small lights with batteries attached, worn on their coats at night, so they could see what money they were taking.'

'Clippie' was one term applied to a female conductor; another was 'conductorette', which conjures up images of being shown to one's seat by a young lady with a torch who might try and sell one an ice cream at the next set of traffic lights. Back in the early 1940s, Essex was clearly far less liberated than it would be 40 years later, for (according to the *Passenger Transport Journal*) the management of Eastern National, which connected with London Transport routes in the Grays and Tilbury

ARP wardens making tea in Brixton Road as a rebuilt ex-Croydon Corporation 'E1' heads south towards Purley, sometime in 1941. *South London Press*

areas, brought in a rule early in 1941 'preventing drivers and conductresses from becoming too friendly'. No fewer than 200 Essex bus men and women threatened to strike, the 'girls contending that their work is … more efficient if they have got used to a particular driver and the driver *has got used to the little peculiarities of their conductorettes*'! (The italics are mine.)

A London tram driver commented that 'In the last war conductresses were not called conductorettes, neither were they dressed in comic opera costumes and hats, but were given proper coats and skirts and knee-length gaiters (providing their own boots), all designed to stand up against the hard and draughty work on a back platform and the perpetual climbing of stairs fitted with steel treads. Slacks made of poor material are not the solution. Wages the same as for men, as the women were doing the same work with equal skill. Women as bus drivers have not "taken on" and a recent picture in the newspapers of young women learning to drive a trolleybus did not make it clear that they were engaged only in shunting. Maybe the bus is too heavy for braking. I remember that in the last war I drove a tramcar with my wife as my conductor and I did not stop at the exact spot at which the more accomplished motormen [stopped], which caused a lady passenger to abuse my poor driving to my conductor with the words:

"Cannot your driver stop when he is told?", to which my conductor replied: "He doesn't do a damn thing he's told — he's my husband!"'

London Transport employed three female clock-winders, Mrs Lily O'Loughlin, Mrs Joan Colvin and Mrs Florence Bex having taken over from men who had gone to war. Its magazine noted that their job was to 'keep 171 clocks going in 52 garages and depots … also at 170 points along the bus and coach routes, conductors record on time-clock cards the time of their arrival.' The ladies travelled by bus around the network, but the 'two skilled fitters' who maintained the clocks had a van, and 'At a moment's notice they can dash off to Leatherhead or Luton to stethoscope a patient whose heart is beating irregularly or not at all.' On St George's Day (23 April) 1942, 12 London women conductors took part in a Battle for Freedom pageant at the Royal Albert Hall. Six worked on the buses, the other six on trams and trolleybuses. For some reason which the account chooses not to divulge, all were 5ft 9in tall — well above average height. They were selected by the Women's Welfare Superintendent, and, as they paraded across the stage of the Royal Albert Hall 'in their summer uniforms of grey-blue, and with their punches flashing, they typified the courage and resolution of the 7,000 such women who have replaced men on the

London Transport vehicles'. They were 'a credit to the Board'.

The employment of female conductors was vital if services were to be maintained. Interestingly the 12,167 employees of the London Passenger Transport Board in the Forces were still paid as though in civilian employment, the LPTB having been granted funds to make up the difference between military and civilian pay. From January 1940 wages were increased, and the rates of tram and trolleybus drivers and conductors were at last raised to equal those of bus crews. There was much resentment of the latter by the former, going way back to the LCC and LGOC days when motor buses were considered (with some justification) to be taking business away from the trams by unfair means, the trams being crippled financially with various charges not imposed on buses. Trams certainly enjoyed a renaissance following the outbreak of war, for it was recorded that in the 12 months from September 1939 'the main operating problems were the rationing of petrol and fuel oil', which meant many buses were taken off the roads whilst trams and trolleybus services were unaffected. Of course, once the Blitz began, every aspect of the LPTB's operations suffered.

One solution to the fuel problem was producer gas. A number of unfortunate petrol-engined STs and Ts had

Gas Producers for London Buses

DEMONSTRATION AT CHISWICK PRIOR TO ENTERING SERVICE

AS mentioned briefly in our last issue, a demonstration of the feasibility of running London Transport buses on gas was given on Tuesday of last week, when a double-deck bus carrying the equivalent of 60 passengers was operated under similar conditions as would be met with in actual service, with the gas producer equipment mounted on a two-wheel trailer.

has been in extensive use under comparable operating conditions.

Anthracite or specially graded coke can be used as fuel for the gas producer. The Board is at present using activated anthracite, activation being the treatment of the fuel with sodium carbonate to increase vehicle performance. When the anthracite fire is lit, the gas given off is passed from the container through cooling

Gas producer trailer fitted to a "S.T." type petrol-engine bus.

During the demonstration, Mr. W. A. C. Snook, the Board's acting chief engineer (buses and coaches), explained that the change-over from petrol to gas must not be confused with a change-over from, say, petrol to paraffin. In this case an ordinary petrol engine, to which certain modifications had been made, was being used as a gas engine with a consequent loss of some 40 per cent. to 50 per cent. in efficiency. In order to reduce this loss the compression ratio has been raised from 5-1 to 8-1 by fitting high compression pistons, thereby reducing the drop in power to some 25-30 per cent. The engine cylinders have been bored out to a larger diameter.

The gas producer unit as used by London Transport for the initial operations has been developed by Messrs. Thomas Tilling Ltd. from the Government emergency producer. Messrs. Tilling have been operating this type for some twelve months, and the Chairman of that Company has very kindly placed at the disposal of London Transport all the experience gained during that period. Fundamentally the only difference from the Government emergency type is that this producer embodies the use of a water filter instead of a Sisal filter. This filter, known as the Morison filter, was introduced and developed by the chief engineer of the Eastern National Omnibus Co. Ltd. This type of producer has been selected by the Board for the reason that for the 7.5 litre engines, as used by London Transport, it was the only one of the required capacity that

chambers into the water filter, and from there through a water separator on the trailer to another on the front of the bulkhead of the bus, then on through a mixing valve to the engine. The method of operation is as follows:

The gas producer has been serviced and properly charged, and is parked away from the bus. The bus

Showing some of the modifications made to the petrol engine to adapt its use for gas.

Above: Britannia and Hitler get admiring glances from a warden corporal as they prepare to set off in a dignified mode of transport to head a parade marking Brixton's Warship Week in 1942. *South London Press*

Far left: An article introducing producer-gas STs. *Passenger Transport Journal*

two-wheel trailers attached which were, in effect, miniature power stations. They burned anthracite treated with sodium carbonate, which produced a gas, and, after various processes this passed through a mixing valve into the engine. Efficiency was down by as much as 50%, and, to help counteract this, the cylinders were bored out to a larger diameter; any attempt to save fuel, at a time when the very continuation of the war was threatened by the huge numbers of tankers being sunk by German U-boats, was worthwhile. The buses were certainly very underpowered, but, by being confined to routes with few or no gradients, they at least kept on the move. In all, 172 STs and nine Ts operated the system between the summer of 1942 and September 1944.

Not everyone — well, possibly no-one — was able to keep a stiff upper lip and act with bravery, compassion and fortitude on every occasion throughout the war. I was sitting on the longitudinal seat downstairs on another ST one afternoon as we pulled away from the Swan & Sugar Loaf at South Croydon (not far from the bus garage) when there was an almighty bang not too far away. 'A bomb!' exclaimed a woman opposite. 'Ah well, that's a few less fares I'll have to bother about,' the conductor replied. It did not go down well with the passengers.

One of the worst consequences of a bomb blast was the shattering of glass. To minimise this risk, netting was stuck on vehicle windows. The trouble was that passengers couldn't see out and immediately began to try and pull it away; on a long journey one could virtually strip a window if one worked assiduously and avoided the conductor's gaze. The solution was to leave a small, clear diamond in the centre, and this worked pretty well. By the end of 1941, 218,400yd of the stuff had been applied — 96,000yd on bus and coach windows, 42,400yd on trams and trolleybuses and 80,000yd on Underground and Tube carriages.

You will want to know precisely how the netting was applied, so here goes, courtesy of the *Passenger Transport Journal*: 'Originally a solution of gum Arabic, plasticised with glycerine, was used but it was found to be subject to condensation and peeled off. The present method is quite satisfactory; the window is given a coating of

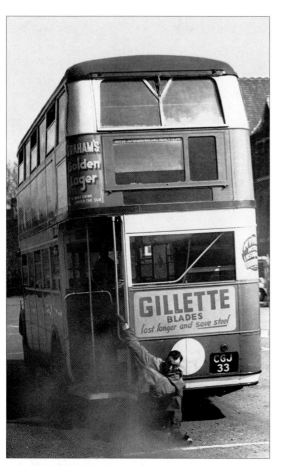

varnish, which is left until it becomes tacky. The netting is then mounted, being first cut to size. A rubber roller is used to press it into position. It is then left overnight to dry. The next day it is given a coating of exterior quality varnish and instead of laying-off with a brush the rubber squeegee is again used. Normally the full process takes two days, but in warm weather it has sometimes been possible to get the two coats on in one day.' We then get the full instructions on how to 'cut the new standard diamond-shaped aperture', but this is altogether too exciting for those of a weak disposition, so we'll merely conclude that the exterior-quality varnish was quality indeed — so much so that, for years after the war, traces of it could still be found on bus, tram and trolleybus windows. (Maybe this would be the solution to graffiti scratched on to the windows of modern-day buses.) Windows continued to be blasted regularly and in large quantities. Glass was just one of the commodities in short supply, and throughout the war it was common to see a London tram, trolleybus or motor bus with many of its windows boarded up.

Left: Don't worry; the unfortunate chap hanging off the back of STL919 was an actor taking part in a children's road safety demonstration at Hackney Downs Secondary School on 16 April 1943. *London Transport*

Below: Workers pour out of their appropriately bucolic-looking factory and board a Watford-based former National ST, still in prewar Country Area dark and light green but with netted windows and white wartime markings. *London Transport*

· 6 ·

Beyond the Blitz

FOLLOWING the triumph of the RAF at the end of the Battle of Britain, daylight raids on London were much reduced, and, whilst the Luftwaffe bombers continued to cause many casualties and much damage at night, this danger also began to reduce, such that by the beginning of 1941 the *South London Press* could claim that, 'whilst London gets routine bombing visits every night, few of them are sufficient to keep Cockneys from their beds'.

One of the delights — and pitfalls — of researching old newspapers is that one inevitably gets sidetracked. I am sure you would like to know that 'Big-Hearted' Arthur Askey and Richard 'Stinker' Murdoch were appearing at the Trocadero, Elephant & Castle — 'Europe's largest cinema' — in *Charley's Aunt*. The two were, along with Tommy Handley, probably the most popular radio comedians of the war years — a popularity that would continue for decades afterwards. The Trocadero was one of the most spectacular of all the magnificent picture palaces erected in the heyday of cinema in the 1920s and '30s. Designed by George Coles, its doors opened in 1930. It boasted a 24-rank Mighty Wurlitzer organ which rose majestically into view and was part of a complete evening's entertainment which included not only the main feature but a second feature, trailers and the Movietone newsreel. The Trocadero had seats for no fewer than 3,500 and

was extremely popular, a welcome diversion from the grim reality of life in the unemployment-hit years of the early 1930s in London's East End. (It would close in October 1963, at a time when television was not only taking millions upon millions away from the cinema but was hitting public transport equally hard, now that people preferred to stay at home and gather round the 'goggle box'.) Alice Faye was simultaneously appearing at the Odeons Camberwell, East Dulwich and Peckham. However, the silver screen was not getting it all its own way, for the Canterbury Music Hall in Westminster Bridge Road, which had been a cinema, was going to revert to variety, once the problem of 'the noise of passing trains' had been solved.

The day would come, decades ahead, when the conductor would be done away with, apart from on a few of the most heavily patronised Central London routes, but even during the depths of the war London Transport was prepared to experiment with variations on the theme of the conductor's traditional role. At this stage there was no notion of getting rid of the conductor, but rather to make the work easier and to ensure that no one got away without paying his/her fare. (The best way of achieving the latter — it pains me to confess — was to make a fairly short journey on a 'Feltham' tram: as the conductor came up the rear stairs, one descended via those at the front and alighted at the

back, one's penny still intact and available for contribution towards that week's *Dandy* or *Beano*.) No pay-as-you-enter experiments were carried out on trams, but two trolleybuses and three motor buses were so adapted. In each the conductor sat at a desk and collected fares as the passengers came aboard. There remained a single entrance/exit, except in the case of STL2284, which had one of each. Four of the vehicles

'Bluebird' LT1403 of Hammersmith (Riverside) garage (R) at the Mitcham Cricket Green terminus of the 88. *Author's collection*

43

Above left: No escaping paying your fare on this 'Feltham'. Looking down the staircase of preserved Feltham No 330. *Author*

Above right: Prototype trolleybus No 61 with Chiswick-built body as converted to experimental pay-as-you-board layout in March 1945. *London Transport*

Left: Passengers paying their fare on pay-as-you-board STL1793. *London Transport*

Above: An evening scene at Waterloo station just before Christmas 1943. One of the Inter Station Leyland Cubs is caught by the flash camera of a Topical Press photographer. The caption reads: 'The first bus leaves from Waterloo station with servicemen and their wives for Paddington'. The Inter Station service was reinstated in December 1943 and was usually worked by STs.
Ian Allan Library

Right: One of the STs repainted into Inter Station blue and cream, at Victoria station. *Alan Cross*

45

One of the many early STLs transferred from the Central to the Country Area and sent to Chelsham garage waits to depart from West Croydon on a summer day towards the end of the war. It retains red livery. *W. J. Haynes*

had suffered bomb damage which made the structural alterations easier. The most interesting, probably, was RT97. A number of the RT class, which had survived the Blitz when brand-new without damage, were casualties in flying-bomb attacks, the worst being RT66, whose body was destroyed in June 1944. The following month RT97 became a casualty, badly damaged when a bomb exploded close by. It was sent to Birmingham to be repaired but was brought back untouched several months later and was then converted at Chiswick for its new role. The only undamaged vehicle used in the experiment was trolleybus No 61, the prototype with a Chiswick-built body; this had a central entrance and was therefore ideal. Powered platform doors were fitted to each vehicle, a circulating space was provided (which resulted in a loss of seating capacity), staircases were moved towards the centre by the entrance, and the conductor issued tickets from a TIM machine.

The experiment failed on several counts. Although no one could get on without paying, it was difficult to check if passengers rode past the stop they had paid for. Passengers themselves, waiting to board, were not best pleased at hanging around at the stop once the bus had arrived whilst other passengers were paying their fares, and loading took longer, which meant schedules were not maintained. The trolleys and two of the buses were rebuilt to see out their days in their original configurations, the exception being RT97, which retained a number of its new features and would, as we shall see, re-emerge after the war as a prototype double-deck coach.

In June 1944 London was suddenly subjected to a new terror, known variously as the flying bomb, 'doodle-bug' or V1. Pilotless aeroplanes launched from France and the Low Countries, these wreaked terrible devast-ation. They *could* be caught by RAF fighters, but if one

got too close and was fired on then the subsequent explosion could bring down the RAF 'craft too. The most satisfactory solution was to fly alongside, put your wingtip under that of the V1 and then flick it over — something its guidance system could not cope with. It would then crash, hopefully into the English Channel or the empty countryside. It could also be brought down by anti-aircraft fire.

It is estimated that around half of all V1s launched against London were destroyed by various methods, but this meant that the other half got through. Bexleyheath trolleybus depot was hit in June 1944. Twelve trolleys were destroyed and nearly all the others damaged, so that for the rest of its time as a trolleybus depot it operated a fleet largely composed of rebuilt or rebodied vehicles. West Ham depot was hit twice, one vehicle being destroyed and over 100 being damaged. Elmers End garage suffered grievously. Seven people died when it received a direct hit from a V1, 32 buses and coaches being completely destroyed and 28 damaged so badly that their bodies were beyond repair.

Between 1939 and 1945 no fewer than 426 London Transport staff were killed, either at work or off duty. The population of Central London generally had, not surprisingly, gone down — by 650,000 — but journeys over the whole of the LT network in 1945 were within 3% of the 1939 total. It was the Country Area which had redressed the balance, its passenger figures almost doubling between 1939 and 1945.

Right: Front page of the *Daily Mail*, 8 May 1945. Two Hendon-based prewar STDs and an LT are caught up in the jubilant celebrations at Piccadilly Circus as the war in Europe comes to an end. *Daily Mail*

Daily Mail

NO. 15,290 ONE PENNY ✱ ✱ FOR KING AND EMPIRE TUESDAY, MAY 8, 1945

VICTORY EDITION

3 POWERS WILL ANNOUNCE GREAT SURRENDER SIMULTANEOUSLY

VE-DAY—IT'S ALL OVER

The King to speak to Empire: Victorious generals will follow Premier on radio

THE pavements and most of the roadways in and around Piccadilly-circus, including Regent-street, were jammed nearly solid for hours yesterday afternoon and evening by crowds expecting to hear VE-Day announced. These Daily Mail pictures give you a vivid impression of the immense concourse of Londoners who waited patiently—and vainly. Other crowd scenes—Page THREE.

Nightcrowd at Palace shouts for the King

West End cheers

By Daily Mail Reporter

LONDON decided to celebrate after all. The crowds flocked back to the West End last night and made VE-Eve whoopee.

Not long after the disappointed thousands had gone home after a day of waiting the streets were full of yelling, singing hordes

In Piccadilly they climbed on to the roofs of buses and taxis.

Outside Buckingham Palace they massed in thousands, and stayed there for hours, chanting "We want the King; We want the King!"

Their shouting and cheering reached crescendo when a plane circled over St. James's Park, just after 10.30 and dropped flares of white, red and yellow.

Cheer leader

A youth clambered to the head of one of the massive stone figures of the monument facing the Palace, and with a foot on each ear led a cheer party in bellowing "G-E-O-R-G-E—We want King George!"

Figures could be seen leaning forward at one of the upper windows, and later someone appeared against the balustrade of the roof. They could not be identified, though an optimistic woman did her best with a pair of binoculars.

Sports cars ran into the thick of the throng, carrying people riding on the mud-guards, radiators, and clinging to the backs. Everywhere there were rattles, squeakers streamers, and paper hats.

A few lights occasionally flickered from the Palace windows. Whenever one was shown from an upstairs room the crowd roared again.

In Piccadilly-circus traffic was stopped. From Leicester-square a huge column, led by Scots piper, marched to join them.

A little man climbed through the upper window of a bus and on to the roof. A New Zealand sailor made a seamanlike trip from the bonnet to join him. A soldier followed—and soon the bus top was perilously packed.

Beer sold out

Soldiers were soon climbing on to the other buses and taxis jammed among the crowd.

Placably, the police shepherded each bus along towards the route it was supposed to follow.

At one time 20 buses were stranded in the centre of the circus.

Most of the public-houses around Piccadilly had to close by 9.30 because they had no more beer.

Cars, nosing along through the crowds, vanished and emerged again with 20 or 30 men and women clinging to the bonnets, the sides, and the back, and others standing on top.

London's Day of Hope—Page THREE.

Lord Lascelles at the Palace

The King's nephew, Lord Lascelles, and the Queen's nephew, the Master of Elphinstone, recently freed from a German prisoners' camp, arrived in London yesterday by plane.

They drove from the airfield to Buckingham Palace, where they were welcomed home by the King and Queen and Princess Elizabeth.

Daily Mail

IN accordance with the expressed desire of the Government that workers generally should enjoy a day's holiday following the announcement of the cessation of hostilities in Europe, the Daily Mail, in common with other London morning newspapers, will not be published on Thursday.

THE WAR GOES ON HERE—

Prague bombed as SS men shoot Czechs

GERMAN bombs are falling on Prague for the first time as the war in Europe enters its last hours. In defiance of surrender orders, German forces in Czechoslovakia are fighting on. They are venting their last spite on the Czechs, shooting them down ruthlessly in the streets of the capital.

Refugees from Prague who have reached Allied-occupied Pilsen say that, in many cases, the S.S. went through the city driving people out of their houses into the streets.

And there other S.S. men mowed them down with machine-guns. The S.S., according to the refugees, know they will probably be executed when caught and have abandoned all normal conduct.

That the S.S. are completely out of hand is indicated in a broadcast by the German commander in Bohemia and Moravia warning his troops to respect international law.

He admitted that "breaches" had occurred among his troops.

Two columns of General Patton's tanks are racing to Prague's rescue and were last reported 15 miles south of the capital.

Pilsen kisses

PILSEN, Monday.

LIEUT.-GENERAL MAJEWLSKI commanding the German garrison of Pilsen, blew out his brains after surrendering with his staff to the U.S. forces who entered the city yesterday. He shot himself with an American automatic in the presence of his wife and staff officers, who tried to talk him out of suicide.

Since Patton's tanks rolled into the city, the population have been dancing with joy and openly singing the Czech national anthem for the first time in six years.

The crowds did not wait for the shooting to stop to begin their singing and dancing and to cheer the American troops. It was just like the liberation scenes in France, with wine, flowers and kisses.—*Reuter.*

Fleet off Oslo

AN Allied naval force of 48 ships has been sighted at the entrance to Oslo Fiord, says the Swedish radio, quoting reports from Oslo.

"There are no reports that troops have been landed, but it is

BACK PAGE—Col. SEVEN

THE WAR'S GREATEST DAY OF SUSPENSE

By WILSON BROADBENT, Diplomatic Correspondent

GERMANY surrendered unconditionally to the Allies yesterday. But there will be no official announcement of victory until 3 p.m. to-day—officially described as VE-Day—when Mr. Churchill will give the news to the world. He will follow this with an address to the House of Commons, and at 9 p.m. the King will speak to Britain and the Empire.

Mr. Churchill's private room at the House of Commons was last night "wired-up" so that if he wishes he can make his broadcast from there.

To-day's announcement will be made simultaneously in London, Washington, and Moscow. To-day, therefore, is the first of the promised two-days V-holiday for the country. Broadcasts will also be made by General Eisenhower and Field-Marshals Montgomery and Alexander.

Mr. Churchill's two statements to-day will not affect his intention to broadcast at length on Thursday night, the fifth anniversary of his assumption of the Premiership.

After the King's speech, London will be floodlighted, searchlights will fill the sky, and it is now possible that there will be a victory salvo of guns, but this point had not been finally settled at a late hour last night.

After his statement in the House of Commons, Mr. Churchill will propose the adjournment of business while M.P.s attend a special Service of Thanksgiving at St. Margaret's Church, Westminster. They will then return to the House of Commons, adjourn, and arrange to meet again on Wednesday.

STANDING BY

Until shortly before 6 o'clock last night it was fully expected that Mr. Churchill would be able to announce the news that the war was over.

He had been standing by the microphone from some time after 3 o'clock, and everything was ready for him to break into the normal programmes of the B.B.C.

Earlier in the day he had been speaking on the Transatlantic telephone to Washington, and he also had several calls to Moscow. His object was to obtain an agreed time for releasing the big news.

There had been a previous agreement that there should be simultaneous times for release. Apparently, in London, it was understood that Monday would be suitable to all concerned.

In anticipation of this important occasion, Mr.

Continued in Back Page, Cols. 4 and 5

SCHACHT SAVED BY 'FIFTH'

Niemoller, too

Daily Mail Special Correspondent

ALLIED H.Q., Italy, Monday.

SOME of the most famous victims of Nazi-ism have been rescued by the Fifth Army from the Prager Wildsee prison camp, near Obblaco, Italy.

Among them was **Pastor Niemoller**, head of the German Confessional Church, whose defiance of Hitler led to a seven years' incarceration in concentration camps.

A few hours after his release Pastor Niemoller held a service in the lounge of a hotel.

His text was the words of Isaiah:

For the mountains shall depart, and the hills be removed; but my kindness shall not depart from thee, neither shall the covenant of my peace be removed, saith the Lord that hath mercy on thee.

In all, the Fifth Army saved 120 hostages, including **Dr. Schuschnigg**, former Chancellor of Austria, who during the week-end was erroneously reported to have been executed by the Germans.

Dr. Schuschnigg's wife was also found. **M. Leon Blum**, former Socialist Premier of France, and his wife, were also freed.

'Evil Hitler'

The camp in which these famous people were found was a smallish affair—a group of huts around a chateau on a hillside. But behind its barbed wire, the Fifth Army men found many high officers—Greek, Russian, Hungarian—and a number of Germans including **Dr. Schacht**, former German Minister of Finance and President of the Reichsbank.

Asked if Hitler was sane, he said: "In some things no, in others he is a genius."

Someone suggested an evil genius, and Schacht said: "Yes, an evil genius . . . an evil and diabolical genius."

None of the prisoners had had any charge preferred against him.

GOEBBELS' BODY IN A SHELTER

Took poison

GOEBBELS, the German Propaganda Minister, his wife, and five children have been found dead in Berlin.

Moscow says that their bodies were found in an air-raid shelter near the Reichstag, and it has been established that all died of poisoning.

No trace has been found of the bodies of Hitler or Göring.

There was speculation in London last night whether the Nazi leaders may have fled to a place of hiding.

It was pointed out, however, that their bodies may have been destroyed in the wreckage of the burning Chancellery or some other building.

MONTY MEETS ROKOSSOVSKY

4 toasts at lunch

TWENTY-FIRST ARMY GROUP Monday. — Field-Marshal Montgomery lunched to-day with Marshal Konstantin Rokossovsky at Wismar.

It was their first meeting, and very cordial greetings were exchanged.

Toasts were drunk to the Allied armies, Mr. Churchill, Marshal Stalin, and President Truman.—*Reuter*

VE-WEATHER

Strait of Dover yesterday: Victory weather, with hours of sunshine. Day temperature, 60deg.; at dusk, 57. Barometer rising.

The U.S. went ahead

'OUR VE-DAY, ANYHOW'

From DON IDDON, Daily Mail Correspondent

NEW YORK, Monday.

THIS was VE-Day in the U.S.—official or not.

The celebrations began in New York at breakfast time, a few minutes after word came from Rheims, France, that Germany had surrendered unconditionally to Britain, the United States, and Russia.

They went on all day despite an avalanche of confused messages, lack of official confirmation, half-denials, and a barrage of rumours that the surrender was a hoax.

The American public, and particularly the New York public, this time was determined that this was the end of the war in Europe, and resolved to commemorate it.

The first reaction, and it was the same all over Manhattan, was to jab open windows, tear up telephone directories, and hurl paper into the streets.

For hours tons upon tons of ticker tape, torn-up newspapers, envelopes, letters, magazines, and in some instances hats and waste-paper baskets, cascaded down.

Tens of thousands of people abandoned work and rushed into the Times-square area, shouting and singing. Motorists blew their hooters, factory whistles shrieked, and in New York Bay ships sounded their sirens.

Bands of Service men and girls paraded the avenues, waving flags, shouting and yelling, planting kisses on strangers, cavorting in and out of bars.

Great stores, offices, the banks, the factories closed down as staffs walked out en masse.

Traffic was completely tied up in mid-town as throngs of gesticulating, laughing people jammed roadways, jumped on to the running-boards of private cars, taxis, and buses.

At first city officials, led by Mayor La Guardia, attempted to curb the jubilation.

Over the radio came a reminder that there was nothing official, that it was merely a report which had declared that war in Europe was over.

The people ignored the advice. They had heard the electrifying report over the radio; they had seen enormous headlines in the extras: "Germany surrenders."

And that was enough.

While New York led the dizzy parade, other cities lagged behind. Washington, the capital, was quiet and the crowd outside the White House small and well-behaved.

Press secretaries said brusquely that when any news was announced it would come from President Truman.

Fanfares

In the Midwest, Chicago took the reports in its stride, did a little mild drinking and half-hearted parading, but kept its head.

These are some of the things that happened in America:

Chefs danced on the awnings of hotels, throwing their stocks of rice and breakfast cereals in handfuls to the crowds below.

Everyone with a trumpet or a saxophone or a trombone opened the windows wide and leaned out, playing a victory fanfare.

Housewives formed up in street parties and marched to the main thoroughfares, clashing frying-pans and saucepan lids.

PATTON 7 MILES FROM PRAGUE

The Patriot Prague radio report that advanced U.S. Third Army tank units have passed the town of Reporyje, about seven miles south of Prague.

BELGIANS TO HEAR CHURCHILL

Brussels radio announces that it is cancelling its transmission for this afternoon so that Belgians can hear Mr. Churchill's speech and listen to B.B.C. broadcasts of London VE-Day

ARRESTED POLES MAY BE TRIED BY LUBLIN

LUBLIN radio said yesterday that the Polish Provisional Government may demand that General Okulicki and others of the 16 Poles arrested by the Russians be tried both in Warsaw and Moscow for high treason.

The radio said: "Public opinion in Poland has received with indignation the news of the action of Okulicki and his accomplices, who are accused of carrying out diversionary activities against the Red Army.

"Because the criminal activities of Okulicki and his accomplices were also directed against the reborn Polish State, it constitutes high treason.

"The Provisional Government reserves the right to demand that Okulicki and his accomplices be turned over to the Polish authorities to be indicted in the courts of the Republic as well."

M. Mikolajczyk, former Polish Prime Minister in London, announced yesterday that he is preparing a statement on the arrests.

He said that the arrested men cannot be accused of diversionary acts against the Soviet forces, as they were sincere partisans of a Polish-Soviet understanding.

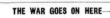

War came to an end twice. The first time, 8 May 1945, was VE Day — Victory in Europe — which was celebrated the day after Germany surrendered; later in the year, on 15 August, came VJ Day — Victory over Japan — after atomic bombs had been dropped on the cities of Hiroshima and Nagasaki.

Having been evacuated to Bournemouth, I missed out on the VE Day street parties, but was back in time for the VJ celebrations. The last bombs — V2 rockets — had fallen on Croydon in January 1945. Taking the tram to the town centre on VJ night, I was enthralled by the spectacle of the Town Hall, the Tudor Whitgift almshouses and other buildings floodlit — something I had certainly never seen before.

The most spectacular parade of all was not held until almost a year after VJ Day. This was the Victory Parade, which took place in Central London on 8 June 1946.

There were actually two parades — one of marching men and women representing all the Allies, and one a mechanical column. I would have preferred to watch the latter but Dad, despite (or perhaps because of) having driven a great variety of military vehicles all over the Middle East between 1914 and 1918, chose the former, and, with the aid of a periscope — a piece of scientific apparatus I had not previously encountered — I had a pretty good view opposite Selfridge's in Oxford Street. We did manage to catch the tail end of the mechanical parade in The Mall, which included two RTs (4 and 39) and two provincial buses (from Manchester and Halifax) which had helped out in London during the war. By this time it had been hoped that the first of London's standard postwar buses — updated versions of the RT — would be in service, but these would not appear for almost a year.

Left: Windsor celebrates the end of the war. Pay-as-you-board STL2284 waits patiently as the crowds watch a marathon which has just started in front of the castle. At the top right of the picture, spanning the street leading to the station, is a 'Victory Day' banner. *London Transport*

Above: The Victory Parade. Crowds line the route, including a servicewoman on the far right, as RT39 and RT4 pass. *F. G. Reynolds*

7

Brave New World

BY late 1944 it was clear that the Allies were winning the war, although no one could predict just when final victory would be achieved. The dropping of the two atomic bombs on Japan ended the war in the Far East more quickly than most had anticipated, but many preparations for the postwar world were already in hand. It might have been thought that London Transport's first priority would be to complete the tram-replacement programme. The tram had been all but swept away from North London: all that remained were the three Kingsway Subway routes (31, 33 and 35), the 34 (which terminated at the end of King's Road, Chelsea), the Victoria routes and, of course, those which ran along the reserved track on the Embankment on the north bank of the Thames. Early in 1946, 77 new trolleybuses were ordered from BUT

(a new name for the well-tried AEC/Leyland combination, the two leading British suppliers of PSV chassis having merged their trolleybus businesses). Forming the 'Q1' class, these vehicles, which had MCW bodywork and were strikingly similar to the prewar fleet, were not the precursors of hundreds more but merely replacements for the original London United 'Diddlers' and wartime losses.

Two reports which came out during the war years prophesied a Corbusier-inspired London of the future, with towering 'cities in the sky' flats and office blocks served by motorways designed for the car, where public transport would be supplied by over- and under-ground railways and motor buses. In this brave new world there would be no need for trams or trolleybuses. London Transport's annual report of 1946 stated that it was

Left: A youth pedalling a three-wheel delivery cycle leads an original STL and a 'Hendon' STD on the southern approach to London Bridge, whilst two standard STLs and an LT head in the opposite direction on 22 October 1946. *London Transport*

Below: On the same day, with headscarves prominent (although with rather less covering on male heads than in prewar days), workers hurry across London Bridge for City offices, with three STs, an STL, a brand-new Series E Morris 8 and a horse-and-cart in the background. The tower of Southwark Cathedral can be seen over the roof of the nearest ST. Also visible is a cargo steamer tied up on the south bank of the river in the Pool of London; London was still the busiest port in the world, and the Pool of London teemed with every type of vessel, including passenger ships working a regular service to Spain, paddle steamers bound for Southend and Ramsgate, as well as cargo ships, barges and lighters. *London Transport*

Many of the later North London ex-corporation cars were transferred south of the river in the late 1930s as their routes were converted to trolleybus operation. One such was No 2054, bought by Walthamstow Corporation in 1932 and seen alongside a Rover of similar vintage at Streatham Hill. These cars were one of the many variations on the 'E1' theme, easily distinguished by their windscreens. Along with the 'Felthams', No 2054 was based at Telford Avenue, some half a mile distant.
Alan Cross

Coombe Road, Croydon. Although only four years separated the building of Croydon Corporation 'E1' No 385 and 'Feltham' No 2192, in concept, appearance, performance and comfort they were light-years apart — which was one of the biggest nails in the tram's coffin. It beggars belief that until the 1930s the LCC and the various corporations could go on building cars which were essentially Edwardian; if they could have got together with the MET and the LUT and invested in fleets based on the Feltham and LCC No 1 concept, the tram would have been able to put up a much better fight.
D. A. Thompson

'essential to select a means of transport not rigidly tied to existing routes'. Any sensible planner knows that transport needs vary, and bus routes in London and its suburbs have always been under review and subject to change; what was not appreciated in the 1940s and '50s is that demand *will* remain more or less constant on certain trunk routes, which is why, in the 21st century, the tram is making a comeback. But in the immediate post-World War 2 period it was decided not only that the tram-replacement programme would continue but also that diesel buses (as opposed to electric trolleybuses) would take the trams' place.

Notwithstanding the aims outlined by LT in 1946, replacement of the trams would have to wait; although shabby and elderly, they were in basically sounder condition than many of the petrol and diesel buses. Even the STL class — London's standard type of the immediate prewar period — was in dire need of almost complete rebuilding. The London bus was not designed to last much more than 10 years, yet the LTs and the STs were well into their teens; wartime neglect meant that many were scarcely roadworthy and would have to be replaced before a start could be made on getting rid of the trams.

A scheme was instituted whereby between November 1945 and October 1949 1,106 prewar buses were overhauled and/or rebuilt by outside contractors. In the early-postwar years all manner of undertakings turned

to building and repairing bus and coach bodies in order to make up for the wartime backlog, most of these firms either reverting to their previous activities or simply disappearing in the 1950s. Mann Egerton of Norwich, hitherto unknown in London-bus circles, carried out most of the work, on 511 STLs, 262 LTs and 29 STs; it would also build completely new single-deck bus bodies on AEC Regal and Leyland Tiger chassis. Redundant wartime aerodromes, with their huge hangars, provided ideal bases for this work. There were many of these in the flatlands of East Anglia, and Mann Egerton sub-contracted much of the work to firms that leased ex-Bomber Command bases.

In most cases the renovation of the double-deckers was not particularly obvious to the casual observer, beyond the fact that they looked in good shape inside and out, and the wartime livery of red and white with a brown roof was retained. However, a number of single-deck Ts and LTs were much more heavily rebuilt by

Marshall of Cambridge, with a general smoothing-out of exterior protrusions and repainting in the new standard all-red livery with narrow cream bands around the windows. They looked rather splendid and, although they retained their original lines (by now going back nearly 20 years), did not appear dated.

There was still considerable shortage of materials, and many buses had to make do with little or no remedial work. Chiswick did a sort of 'parcels' effect, wrapping strengthening straps around members of the STL class, a bit like a mini mediæval buttress. This did nothing to beautify vehicles, but it kept them on the road until new members of the RT family could put them out of their misery. A few vehicles were disposed of, notably the four remaining double-deck Qs, (Nos 2, 4, 5 and 188). These revolutionary buses had not run since the outbreak of war and were too non-standard to justify the time and expenditure required to keep them on the road. Q3 had been damaged in an air raid in 1941 and was

The most dramatic rebuild of any prewar bus (in terms of appearance, at least) was carried out on LT1131, by Bush & Twiddy of Norwich — a name not readily associated with London buses.
In the distance is a Weymann-bodied TD.
Ian Allan Library

subsequently scrapped, but the others found new owners. Q2 ended its days as a snack bar, having been converted by St Helens to a single-decker, Q4 went to Blue Ensign of Doncaster, which ran it until 1951, whilst Q5 and the six-wheeled Q188 migrated (as would many more London double-deckers) to Scotland, being operated until c1950 by H. Brown of Garelochhead. Q188 had still not come to the end of its career, for it then re-emerged as a furniture van and continued to work in the Cheshire area until 1953. One or two other double-deck Qs lasted in passenger service but none survived to be preserved. The best we can do is buy one of the handsome Corgi models of Q2 or Q3, or make a pilgrimage to visit the preserved single-deck versions.

Meanwhile orders were put in for some 500 of the postwar standard double-decker, the RT. In fact 338 RTs, in addition to the initial 151, had been ordered at the end of 1938, but, of course, the war had put a stop to this. Chiswick Works had so many other demands placed upon it that there was no capacity to build new bodies, so the contract for these was awarded to Park Royal and Weymann. But 1946 came and went, and there was as yet no sign of the new bus. Deliveries of wartime Bristols, Guys and Daimlers were completed in that year, the last examples being rather less austere than their predecessors, and a small number of new AEC and Leyland double-deckers, to more-or-less full peacetime specification, also arrived. They were also of purely provincial design.

Bristol began bus production again in 1945 and London Transport was allocated 20 K6As. With their AEC engines and less than totally austere Duple 56-seat bodywork they were by no means the least popular of

the wartime buses. They had the elegant, low, standard postwar radiator and spent their lives working out of Hanwell garage. Upon disposal by London Transport in the early 1950s they were snapped up by the Tilling Group and, rebodied, continued at work for some years. The final 100 Daimlers were also of an interim nature. Their Park Royal bodies were almost of prewar appearance; they had full three-piece route indicators back and front (although these were never fully utilised), and their seats were trimmed with standard LT moquette. All 100 were allocated to Sutton garage, and thus the Sutton/Morden/Mitcham area became very much Daimler-land.

Twenty AEC Regent Is fitted with handsome 56-seat Weymann bodies arrived at the end of 1945 and were put to work from Watford garage in early 1946 on routes 321/351. Not all were in Country Area livery initially, but they were soon repainted and all wore the green and white with brown roof of the immediate prewar and wartime years. In contrast, 65 all-Leyland PD1s which arrived around the same time were painted in the standard early-postwar Central Area livery of red with a cream waistband and upper-deck window frames. A few worked from my home garage, Croydon, and passed the end of our road whilst carrying out their duties on the very suburban 115 route, linking Wallington with Croydon Airport. Croydon's STDs soon took themselves off northwards. The class was a familiar sight in and around Victoria, a number living at Gillingham Street garage, working the 10, 38 and 38A.

Both the Weymann-bodied AEC Regent and the all-Leyland Titan — two classic designs — could be seen the length and breadth of the land. Very little concession

Above: One of the later and very different-looking Guys, G281 was fitted with a Northern Counties body — much more rounded than other wartime designs. It arrived in 1945 and is seen here in Chingford, an excellent venue for G-class-spotters. *R. E. Vincent*

Right: G153 of 1945 seen in Prestons Road, Wembley, alongside a Bedford lorry of similar vintage. *F. G. Reynolds*

Left: One of the final group of 100 Daimlers, Sutton garage's D208, with semi-austerity Park Royal bodywork, at Morden. It is in the early-postwar livery of all-over red with two narrow cream bands. *Alan Cross*

was made to LT requirements in either case. The STLs had a basic single-piece front indicator and nothing at the back, and, whilst the STDs were fitted with a prewar STL-type full front destination and 'via' indicator with a roof-mounted number box, the actual display was still the restricted wartime standard; approaching an STL or an STD from the rear, you had to guess where it was going unless you managed to catch a glimpse of the minuscule number stencil as you steamed in pursuit. In other respects both types were a huge improvement on the austerity types with which Londoners had had to contend throughout the 1940s. There was a return to peacetime interior standards of trim and seating, and, at £2,593, an STL was actually £96 cheaper than an austerity D — a real bargain.

The year 1946 saw the reinstatement of the Green Line network. The first routes, with their new 7xx-series numbers, were the 715 (Hertford–Oxford Circus–Guildford) and the 720 (Aldgate–Bishop's Stortford), which started on 6 February, and by June the complete service was up and running and doing excellent business. The 'demobbed' 10T10s, the TFs and the Qs worked all the routes except for the particularly heavily patronised services east from Aldgate, which employed (believe it or not) 37 austerity Daimlers. Any pretence that Green Line routes were operated by what the rest of the world thought of as coaches had been well and truly abandoned.

Initially many of the Green Line coaches carried the livery of green and off-white worn by Country Area buses, but the off-white was soon replaced by a distinguishing pale green. Route boards were carried on the sides above the windows, and from 29 May distinctive new blinds were fitted front and rear, featuring black lettering on a yellow-orange background, described officially as 'old gold'.

Right: The final additions to the STL class were the provincial-style Weymann-bodied Regents of 1945/6. Newly delivered STL2687 of Watford High Street garage is seen out in the Hertfordshire countryside. *Author's collection*

Left: King's Cross in 1946. In the foreground a 'prewar' RT heads westwards; behind 'B2' trolleybus No 118 is preparing to turn right to head northwards between St Pancras and King's Cross stations. In the other direction are a 'sit-up-and-beg' STL, another one of the original RTs, a CR (helping out in these days of acute vehicle shortage), a further STL and a trolleybus. *London Transport*

Below: Still in LNER territory, a newly delivered STD-class Leyland PD1 of Loughton garage waits for an 'N7' 0-6-2T to pass with a suburban stopping train. *London Transport*

9T9 T406 being restored to Green Line livery after war service as an ambulance. Livery is green and white, and the indicator has white lettering on a black background — two short-lived, early-postwar features. The 9T9s put in little Green Line work, being considered underpowered compared to the 10T10s, and saw out their days as Country Area buses. *London Transport*

Backbone of the Green Line fleet in the early postwar period was the handsome 10T10 class. T687, resplendent in the new two-tone green livery with black-on-amber route blinds, poses near Godstone for its official picture on a foggy winter morning in 1946. *London Transport*

The first single-deckers since the CRs arrived in 1946. Like contemporary double-deckers these were more-or-less-standard provincial AECs and Leylands, although all were fitted with virtually identical bodywork by Weymann. The 50 AEC Regals were, naturally enough, added to the T class, while the 31 Leyland Tigers started off a new TD class (the prewar TD class of early Leyland Titans having become extinct in 1939). All 81 were painted in the new livery of red with a thin cream band above and below the windows.

All sorts of sporting events not held since the declaration of war came back — welcome signs of peace and stability returning. Charlton, with Sam Bartram in goal, won the FA Cup, no doubt cheered on by many employees of the Central Tram & Trolleybus

D161, one of the very early postwar Daimlers used on the East London Green Line services, in this instance the 722 to Upminster, at Aldgate bus station. Two TFs are in the background. *Alan Cross*

CR47 helps out on the 88, normally the preserve of vastly bigger LTs, as it speeds across the tram tracks at Tooting Broadway. *Author's collection*

Repair Depot, and Dad and I went to watch the Boat Race. For some reason we supported dark-blue Oxford, which didn't do them any good, as they were soundly beaten by Cambridge, but it was all very exciting, especially walking back along the Upper Richmond Road to catch a 630 trolleybus home from Putney, and watching what seemed like practically half the entire fleet of original RTs pass by, each one packed to the gunwales.

T768, the final member of the 50 provincial-style 14T12s, with Weymann 33-seat bodywork of 1946, at Greenford. *Author*

· 8 ·

The Long Haul out of Austerity

AS we all know, we British love discussing our weather. Whenever it decides to do anything which we perceive out of the ordinary we complain bitterly that we've never had to suffer so much cold/wet/heat/ice/snow/sun/lack of sun/etc. We blame God/the atomic bomb/the Health Service/global warming/the state of English cricket/modern youth/etc, feel a lot better and then go about our business. Well, in 1947 we really did, for once, have cause for complaint.

For most of January there was little indication of what was about to descend on Britain; indeed, the weather was unusually mild, lulling us into a false sense of well-being. On the night of the 20th there was a frost — nothing unusual, you might think, for mid-winter, but on the 23rd it began to snow with a vengeance. From

then until 17 March it snowed every day somewhere in the United Kingdom. Central London, which is always that much warmer than its immediate surroundings (to say nothing of the polar regions north of Watford) suffered less than much of the country, but it was bad enough all the same.

February was awful. For 22 consecutive days Kew recorded no sunshine at all; when it did break through, the night-time temperatures plummeted, and in the far north of London Transport's Country Area, around Luton and Dunstable, it fell to –4°F (–20°C). Inevitably, in the outer suburbs and the Home Counties, particularly the hills of the Chilterns and the North Downs, where the snow lay deepest, bus services suffered more disruption than those closer in to the capital, but every part of the network was affected. Snow and ice penetrated the tram conduit, and services ground to a halt, although disruptions seldom lasted more than an hour. Staff worked heroically to clear a way. No fewer than 50 tram and 120 trolleybus motors suffered snow damage, and hundreds of motor-bus radiators cracked. Everywhere Britain slowed down and in parts almost ground to a halt. Coal could not get through, people stayed at home, electricity supplies were affected and production stalled, which meant the delivery of the long-promised RTs was further delayed.

March offered no respite. High winds and snowstorms meant heavy drifting, the snow reaching a depth of 10ft in the Chilterns. On 10 March it looked as if the worst was over, for the temperature began to rise as mild air came in from the south-west. In reality this simply heralded another hefty swipe from vengeful Nature: the resulting sudden thaw brought even more dramatic conditions, with melting snows and ground still frozen from weeks of frost causing extensive flooding in the Thames Valley, services around Windsor

Rehabilitated former Croydon Corporation 'E1' tram No 380 in freezing conditions on the Embankment in February 1947.
Ian Allan Library

Although this picture of 'N1' trolleybus No 1594 was taken at Paddington Green a decade or so later, it illustrates the conditions London Transport had to contend with during the winter of early 1947. *Author*

'E3' No 1927 at Hackney while working the 31, one of the three Kingsway Subway routes which continued to penetrate deep into North London in postwar days. *Author's collection*

Above: Weymann-bodied RT428 (of Leyton) and a milk cart cross LNER tracks in Leytonstone. Deliveries of bread, greengroceries and especially milk by horse-and-cart were an everyday sight in London when the first postwar RTs were new.
London Transport

Right: Park Royal-bodied RT251 of Bromley, on its way to Croydon. The route number on the lower deck (above the garage code) was a short-lived feature of the early postwar RTs.
F. G. Reynolds

and Staines being particularly hit; Watford High Street garage had to be abandoned for two days until it dried out. A deepening depression which reached southern England on 16 March brought high winds, reaching 80-90 knots and inflicting yet more (if varied) misery on the long-suffering populace, which was having to endure shortages of everything from coal to food as all forms of communication were disrupted. A final flourish was rain on an almost unprecedented scale. Camden Square recorded no less than 122 hours of it in March, making this the third-wettest month in London since records began in 1881.

Spring brought vastly happier tidings. Saturday 10 May 1947 is a significant date in the history of London's public transport, for it was then that the postwar RT — regarded by many as the finest piece of urban road transport ever — entered public service. RT402 (HLX 219) was delivered to Leyton garage and took up work that day on the 10 (Woodford Bridge–Victoria) and could thus be seen at the capital's best-known bus terminus. It was undeniably a thing of beauty and stood out from the rather down-at-heel crowd all around it. RT402 had a Weymann body; on 23 May it was joined by RT152 (HLW 139), with Park Royal body. These two manufacturers would supply the vast majority of bodies to London Transport in the next seven years. So closely did they follow the guidelines laid down by London Transport that it was virtually impossible to distinguish a Park Royal from a Weymann body; they were interchangeable, even (in later years) between AEC and Leyland chassis. It took a real rivet counter to

distinguish one from the other, and not even John Wadham or Clive Gillam — my mentors in all things London Transport in Class Five at Winterbourne Primary School — could enlighten me. The buses they replaced were the oldest, open-staircase LTs, which were almost 20 years old, having nearly doubled their expected life span. However, these did not immediately stagger off to the scrapyard, for quite a few of them were in rather better condition than their newer, enclosed-staircase brethren and even many of the later STLs, so they were sent to a variety of Central Area garages to hold the fort until the trickle of postwar replacements became a flood. London Transport was having to operate 2.6% more services (in terms of route mileage) than in 1939, and, whilst this may not sound much, given the size of the London network it required several hundred extra vehicles.

By the end of 1947 171 new RTs were in service. When one considers the size of LT's fleet — and the size of its problems in dealing with the decrepit and time-expired — this was nothing like enough. So what was to be done? Someone must have consulted the ghost of Marie Antoinette and decided that if there was no bread to be had then Londoners had better be

Right: B18, a Duple-bodied Bristol of 1945/6 at Ealing. Is that the Queen Mother, behind the lady encumbered with pram and children, about to board? *F. G. Reynolds*

Below: ST802 intrudes into Daimler land on the forecourt of Morden station. *Alan Cross*

Above: T207, one of the pioneer Green Line coaches, seen in its declining years working as a bus from Kingston garage. Behind stands a Cravens-bodied RT, which type had just replaced the original 60-seat STLs on the 65. *F. G. Reynolds*

Left: One of the many exchanges between the Central and Country Areas features once-green BRCW-bodied Q53, transferred to Kingston garage and repainted red. It is seen being pursued through Kingston by a refurbished T17. *D. W. K. Jones*

offered cake, as luxury coaches were now provided for the lucky few to take them to work and fetch them home again. Others had to make do with a wartime austerity normal-control Bedford OWB or a relic from the 1920s in the shape of a Gilford or a very early Leyland Tiger — or perhaps even a Midland Red-built SOS, which certainly looked like a relic from a bygone age, even if these looks were slightly deceptive.

What the LPTB decided to do was hire in several hundred vehicles from coach operators in the Greater London area. Not surprisingly, only two years after the end of the war these varied enormously, from brand-new Duple- and Harrington-bodied Leyland Tigers, AEC Regals and Dennis Lancets to second-, third- and umpteenth-hand representatives of practically every variety of PSV produced in the UK over the previous 20-odd years. The latter even included some ex-London Transport buses and coaches disposed of but now temporarily returned to mother, among them the prototype Leyland Cub (C1) and Leyland Tiger (TF1). In the middle of October the vehicles were brought to Chiswick for inspection, and the engineers must really have got their skates on, for by Monday 27th 325

coaches were ready to take up work. Many of these were far from suitable for Central London bus duties, but they were better than nothing. Two faults were common to most vehicles — limited capacity and coach-type seating. Getting in and out was not easy, but many of them were rather more comfortable than a London double-decker, and if one was travelling a fair distance — in from the suburbs to Central London to work, for instance — then such a journey could be a distinctly pleasurable experience. The scheme must have been considered successful, for the original contracts were extended beyond 1947 and throughout 1948, not finishing until August 1949. In all some 550 coaches took part, with their owners providing the drivers.

A fascinating pair of coaches helping out London Transport's vehicle shortage at Victoria, with an RT and a G behind. On the left is a Gilford 168OT of Elms, Phillips & Brown of Tottenham, dating from 1933; next to it is a Leyland Tiger TS1 of 1930, re-registered and fitted with later 'Covrad' radiator, of Vineys, also of Tottenham. *Alan Cross*

· 9 ·

Nationalisation

RTL501, the first of its class and the only one to be built with a roofbox body, heads westwards towards Hounslow in an area which was gradually becoming dominated by the ever-expanding Heathrow. *Author's collection*

ON 1 January 1948 London Transport, along with the four main-line railway companies, was nationalised. Lord Ashfield, who, with Frank Pick had put London Transport at the forefront of innovation, had quit as Chairman in October 1947 to join the British Transport Commission. He died before the year was out. The legal lettering on vehicles now read 'London Transport Executive', but, as far as the travelling public was concerned, very little changed. Behind the scenes, the world *had* changed, however, for London Transport no longer had the freedom it had enjoyed under Ashfield and Pick, and the BTC was responsible for major decisions.

Rationing would persist right through the 1940s, and there would be shortages of all manner of items — not least Hornby train sets and Dinky Toys — but the world was gradually recovering from the terrible years of World War 2. The unemployment of the 1930s was replaced by the opportunity for every able-bodied member of society to help produce for a world eager for virtually anything Britain could make. 'Export or die' was the cry, and the slogan 'Britain can make it' was often modified or added to by a workforce which looked

longingly at all the consumer items it now had the money to buy but which were whisked off to earn much-needed foreign currency. Petrol was still rationed, and most new cars were shipped off to the Empire (or Commonwealth, as it was now starting to be called), as well as Europe and (in the case of high-powered sports cars) the USA. On 1 June 1948 petrol, although strictly rationed, became available to the private motorist. Dad was at last able to get our 1932 Lanchester 10 (which he had bought from the front garden of a house on Brixton Hill for £3 10s in 1943) on the road. Our first expedition was to Reigate Heath, where I watched Qs and STLs pass on the A25 and a brand-new Southdown Leyland Tiger PS1 arrive on an evening excursion from Brighton. The Lanchester would be sold later when my twin sisters arrived — 'Can't afford all three,' as Dad put it — but the boost to private motoring heralded a world where the ownership of a car would become the norm for most families, with all that would mean for public transport.

AEC and Leyland were at the forefront of the export drive, but by 1950 they were able to satisfy many home needs. Production of the RT soared, and in June 1948 the Leyland version appeared in the shape of RTL501.

Above: Outside the impressive Horniman Museum in Forest Hill, 'HR2' No 1859 heads for the steep, four-track section at Dog Kennel Hill, Dulwich, on one of the hilly routes for which these ex-LCC cars were specifically designed. *Author's collection*

Right: Most of the Croydon Corporation 'E1s' spent their entire careers on home territory. No 393 stands at the Purley terminus of the 16/18 — the most southerly point reached by London trams. The conductor keeps a watchful eye as his passengers alight in the middle of the road whilst a Ford V8 Pilot waits to pass — one of the hazards of tram travel, and a powerful argument at that time for its abolition. The indicator is already set for its return journey; the conductor will shortly lower the far pole and raise that at this end, after which No 393 will set off back to Croydon behind the RT. *A. W. V. Mace*

This curious number was arrived at on account of its being intended that the first 500 should be 8ft wide, unlike the hitherto-standard 7ft 6in.

It will be recalled that 8ft-wide trolleybuses had been diverted from South Africa to London during the war, and now a batch 8ft wide and built to London specification arrived. These were the 'Q1s', ordered in 1946. Aside from their extra width (which gave them a somewhat tubby appearance) and the five- (instead of six-) side-window layout, they were otherwise remarkably like the last standard prewar 'P1' trolleys. The 'Q1s' were sent to Fulwell and throughout their careers were associated with the Kingston area.

The first production batch of RTLs comprised buses

No 1838, one of the 1948 delivery of 8ft-wide 'Q1' trolleybuses, at Tolworth — an area always associated with these vehicles. *Author*

not to the promised 8ft width but to the previous standard, and had bodies identical to the latest RTs. Right through the 1930s no one seemed to be quite sure how route indicators should be arranged — or maybe it was that several people had very definite ideas, and each was allowed to try his out. At any rate, a standard seemed to have been reached with the newest STLs. In these the number indicator was in the roof, and the destination was above the 'via' point. The 'prewar' RTs continued with this, but the first postwar examples had the destination below the 'via' indicator. Even this was not the final variation, however, for RT852 appeared at the 1948 Commercial Motor Show with the number

STLs, a 'Hendon' STD and a 3RT3/1 without roofbox in Trafalgar Square in 1949. *Alan Cross*

indicator removed from the roof and placed alongside the 'via' display, to its right (identical to the rear layout of the standard STL), the body being designated RT3/1. One reason for this change was said to be that the roof was weakened by the roofbox (although, to my knowledge, no owner of a preserved STL or RT with this arrangement has ever detected any problem). Henceforth the new layout was adopted as standard, and the Park Royal bodies on the first production RTLs perpetuated the RT3/1 design.

No fewer than 1,200 new buses were expected in 1948; in the event there were 755 RTs and RTLs. By the standards of any other undertaking, even this would have been quite enormous, but it wasn't sufficient to satisfy London Transport's needs. Prewar buses were falling by the wayside in unsustainable numbers, and so

Above: RT683 passing Tottenham Court Road tube station, followed by a wartime Daimler. *Ian Allan Library*

Top right: This lowbridge ECW-bodied Bristol K (Eastern National 4007) looks as if it only just fits under the bridge at Waterloo, but of course there was (and remains) sufficient clearance for normal-height double-deckers. *Alan Cross*

Lower right: A highbridge ECW-bodied Bristol K6A destined for Eastern Counties finds itself working from Potters Bar garage in 1949. *Ian Allan Library*

on 7 December 1948 five extraordinary, brand-new apparitions materialised in the shape of lowbridge ECW-bodied Bristol Ks — three red and two green. Like London Transport, Bristol and ECW were part of the British Transport Commission, and thus 180 Bristol double-deckers, instead of being delivered to their Tilling Group owners, were sent to London.

The Bristol Ks were tough and well-built (if a trifle unsophisticated by London standards), their chief disadvantage in London, where there were few constraints on vehicle height, being their lowbridge layout. There were a few highbridge examples, intended for Brighton, Hove & District and for Eastern Counties, but the great majority were 55-seat lowbridge examples with four seats abreast upstairs (making the conductor's work more difficult) and a sunken gangway on the offside, which projected into the lower deck and was skilfully designed to catch the head of any unwary passenger larger than a dwarf. All in all these were not the most popular vehicles ever to have been foisted upon London's travelling public. Of course, to schoolboys like myself they were a fascinating variation on the norm, and for me brought back the days when I used to travel on Hants & Dorset examples in 1944 and early 1945. Indeed, some Hants & Dorset AEC-engined K6A buses did run in London, and Corgi makes an excellent model of TD895 (HLJ 44) with blinds set for working the 336 from Chesham to Watford.

I once had a ride on a highbridge example based at Croydon garage on the 68 — the only one I can remember. Records state that they also worked the 166 and 166A, but I rather doubt this, for these routes passed the top of our road. I was a regular user of both and would surely have remembered any journey on such an unusual bus. But then again, memory can play tricks.

The final total of Tilling buses, purloined from their rightful owners, was 45 highbridge examples (all from Brighton or Eastern Counties) and 135 lowbridge, all being in service by 16 June 1949. They were due to pass to their rightful owners between the end of 1949 and the middle of 1950, which was more or less what happened, although the dispersal rate was somewhat slower than originally intended — another indication that wartime depredations were not yet overcome.

Not even 550 coaches and 180 Bristols could totally satisfy London's desperate need for buses — in 1948 London Transport carried 4,675,000,000 passengers, its greatest total ever — and in 1949 three almost-new Daimler CVG6 double-deckers were hired from Maidstone Corporation and 17 prewar AEC Regents from Leeds.

Top left: One of the few double-deckers hired by London Transport was this centre-entrance, Brush-bodied AEC Regent of 1931, owned originally by Burnley, Colne & Nelson Corporation. *Author's collection*

Lower left: T769, one of the final examples of the many varieties of the T class, the 15T13 of 1948, does excellent business at Hemel Hempstead. *F. G. Reynolds*

Right: One of the Brush-bodied Daimlers borrowed from Maidstone Corporation at work from Sutton garage under the trolleybus wires — as it would have been back home. *Author's collection*

Below: Sent to ease London's chronic shortage of buses in the immediate postwar years, a new ECW-bodied Bristol K, destined for Hants & Dorset but working from Godstone garage, finds itself at Bromley about to set off for Biggin Hill, Westerham, Oxted, Redhill and Reigate. Unlike most of the lowbridge Tilling Group double-deckers, this one was appropriately employed on a route normally worked by lowbridge STLs. *Alan Cross*

10

Ends and Beginnings

THE need for vehicles from unlikely sources was driven by the very poor condition of the prewar fleet. Buses were regularly inspected and, if they failed to pass a roadworthiness test, were marked with the inscription 'PSV71' and had to be withdrawn and sent for scrap. Bodywork was usually the determining factor; no London bus was intended to last more than 10 years, yet here they were struggling on way beyond this. Many mechanical parts were also being expected to last much longer than normal.

The year 1948 also saw the delivery of London Transport's last half-cab single-deckers. The final members of the T class, nearly 20 years newer than the original members, were 30 Regal IIIs, of the 15T13 variety. Painted green and (anachronistically) white, they were put to work in the Country Area. They were immediately followed by 100 TD-class Leyland Tiger PS1s; these were given the new standard livery of all-red with a cream line above and below the windows and were sent to a number of garages, enabling a few (but not many, there being a shortage of single-deckers) elderly members of the T and LT classes to be

withdrawn. The new Ts and TDs all had Mann Egerton bodies, identical except that the Ts had sliding passenger doors and the TDs none. Mann Egerton had never previously built bus bodies for London but had built up vast experience of refurbishing STs, LTs and STLs. Although officially stated to be of provincial design, these single-deckers always seemed to me to incorporate many Chiswick features, and I know of no others in service outside London. There are preserved examples of each type, so the reader can judge for him/herself.

As part of the planned extension of the Northern Line beyond Edgware, a large depot had been built out in the country at Aldenham. The extension had not yet taken place (and in fact never would), so the depot was 'temporarily' adapted to deal with buses. This arrangement would soon become permanent: a production line was set up, and all heavy body repairs and overhauls were transferred there away from the garages and from Chiswick. It became as much a Mecca for enthusiasts as Chiswick — and equally difficult to enter without permission. The best most could do in later years was to sit through endless replays of the Cliff

Above: Rehabilitated 'E1' No 1422 has the streets immediately south of Southwark Bridge virtually to itself, the curve of which can be seen in the distance, with the façade of City offices beyond. Even today, Southwark's is much the least-used of all the London bridges. Commencing its journey on the north bank of the river, the 46 wended its way through South East London before ending up back beside the Thames at Woolwich. *D. A. Thompson*

Far left: Among this fascinating collection of vehicles in the Holloway Road are four 'E3' trams, at least two STs, two STLs, a lowbridge ECW-bodied Bristol and a trolleybus. *Ian Allan Library*

Left: An 'E3' tram with an RT in the distance amongst the shoppers on a sunny day in Woolwich in 1949. *R. Hubble*

Right: A group of time-expired STs and one STL at Epsom Racecourse for the 1949 Derby. Military uniforms are still prominent. *Author's collection*

Below: Members of the Lebanese Olympic team alight from a CR at Wembley in the summer of 1948. *Ian Allan Library*

Richard & the Shadows film *Summer Holiday*, wherein an RT was taken on a European excursion and featured an extensive musical sequence where the bus (several, actually) is prepared for immortality as it is taken through the various stages of overhaul at Aldenham.

Within the weather — not as ferocious as the previous year — there still lurked a vicious streak, heavy snowfalls towards the end of February 1948 closing a number of roads across the North Downs and causing several days' disruption to Country Area services worked by Chelsham and Dunton Green garages.

Once spring arrived there was great demand on the Green Line and Country Area bus routes — places such as Whipsnade Zoo, Windsor and the Surrey Hills proving very popular — and 141 buses were borrowed from the Central Area. Ken Glazier, in his book *Routes to Recovery* (Capital Transport, 2000), recalls that on Easter Monday it was 3pm before all those wishing to leave Victoria Coach Station for Windsor could get away. Demand was even greater with the warmer weather and longer evenings of Whitsun. Central Area buses increased their revenue by 15% over the same period in 1947, Epping Forest and the Thames at Richmond and Hampton Court being particular favourites, whilst there was a similar situation further out into the rural Home Counties, where Country Area buses were doing equally well: Green Line takings were up by a staggering 25%. London Transport would never have it so good again. Not surprisingly, many of the coach operators which had lent their vehicles to London Transport wanted them back. Over 100 were returned but only 63 were obtained from other operators. None was used by London Transport at weekends; although they would have been ideal for such work, there was an agreement that LT would not use them to compete with their owners.

Having clearly got the bit between its teeth, the weather had yet more surprises in store and on 14 June unleashed thunderstorms of such violence that 37 East London trolleybuses had to be taken out of service on account of flood damage.

To help deal with extra seasonal demands a 'Special Events' fleet was formed, consisting of some 50 more-or-less time-expired buses — principally STs and LTs — which, whilst not fit for regular daily passenger service, could just about stagger up the hill from Morden or Epsom station to Epsom Racecourse on Derby Day or from Wimbledon station to the All England Lawn Tennis Club; a number of driver-training buses also remained licensed for such work.

In the summer of 1948 London hosted the first postwar Olympic Games. Although this put huge demands on an already stretched transport system the event was generally welcomed, for it was a very visible sign that the world was returning to normality after the horrors of the war. The main venue for the Games was Wembley Stadium, but events took place at football and

LT91 of the Special Events fleet waits outside Wimbledon station for customers for the Lawn Tennis Championships in June 1949. *Alan Cross*

sports grounds all over the London area. London Transport simply didn't have the capacity to lay on many extra vehicles, the exception being the 662 trolleybus route from Paddington to Wembley, which was boosted to 10 trolleys an hour using vehicles displaced by the new 'Q1s'. The Underground carried most of the traffic, whilst some 30-odd single-deckers, mostly LTC six-wheeled coaches and the unreliable CR-class 20-seat rear-engined Cubs, were provided for competitors. At the peak of the Games, double-deckers — a mixed bag of due-to-be-retired LTs and STs and brand-new RTs — ferried competitors to and from Wembley.

The first RTs to be delivered to the Country Area took up work in the northern area — on the 301 from Tring and Two Waters (Hemel Hempstead) garages — on 21 July 1948. Numbered in the 5xx/6xx series and with HLX registrations, they were known to us bus spotters only from the Ian Allan 'ABCs', and we longed to see a real one for ourselves. They first reached the southern area at the end of the summer, when three

Left: A 3RT3 leads an ST and an STL around Trafalgar Square in 1949. *Author's collection*

Below left: ST16 of Alperton garage stands outside the Empire Pool, Wembley, in 1948. *Author's collection*

Above: A shiny new Country Area RT650, devoid of adverts, seen in Watford in 1948. *Author's collection*

Below: At London Bridge in 1948, brand-new 3RT8 RT1118 prepares to set off for the northern extremities of the Central Area. *Author's collection*

Top left: LTs were still working the 38 when this picture was taken at Victoria in May 1949, but the new RT alongside LT285 indicates that the latter's days were numbered. *Alan Cross*

Lower left: An outside-staircase LT, looking pretty good despite its 19 years, awaits business behind a Tilling ST. *Forever Amber — Blue Peter* material today — was considered scorching, red-hot stuff in 1948. *Alan Cross*

Above: An LT and a standard STL meet their end at a scrapyard in Rainham in June 1949. Although the Fox Photos caption describes STL2028 as 'ancient' it was actually a mere 12 years old, having been delivered to Holloway garage in March 1937. *Ian Allan Library*

went to Leatherhead. This garage had a share in the 408 and the 470, which served our part of the world, but for a while the new RTs kept well away, on the 418. Eventually, just before the year was out, we got our first sight of these (for a few weeks) advert-less beauties, when more were delivered to Leatherhead and to Reigate. By now JXC and JXN registrations had taken over from the HLXs.

STs and LTs were now disappearing fast. Old, faithful friends and (in the case of the LTs in particular) full of character though they were, they compared very badly

with the magnificent new RTs and RTLs. LT1, dating from August 1929, whilst certainly not the first to go, was taken out of service in November 1948, and a few other open-staircase versions lasted into 1949. London Transport, more than any other transport undertaking, was aware of its heritage, and LT165 and ST821 were put aside for preservation. They were stored for a number of years at Reigate garage, where we spotters naturally converged in the hope of catching a glimpse of these and other hidden-away veterans. It would be a long time before they appeared permanently in public.

Above: Part of tram route 12 was converted to trolleybus 612 in 1937; the intention was that the entire route should be operated by trolleybuses once the south-side tram routes were replaced, but the war intervened and the 12 continued to run between Wandsworth and the Borough until 1950, when both it and the 612 were replaced by motor-bus route 44. This is 'D3' No 514 of Wandsworth depot. *Author's collection*

Left: On loan to the Country Area, red ST374, one of 10 built with this type of route indicator, heads through South Croydon for Redhill in the summer of 1949, performing one of its last duties before withdrawal. *Author's collection*

Above: A pair of STLs in the red and cream standard in postwar years until all-red became the norm. STL1780 leads STL1243 at Redbridge station. *R. E. Vincent*

Right: One of the many variations in the LT class was this one, seen at Victoria shortly before withdrawal. The indicator is mounted directly over the driver's cab, but above it is provision for a board with further details and illuminated at night by the lamp set into the upper-deck central window frame. Board and lamp were taken out of use in the early years of the war and never reinstated. *Author's collection*

11

RT Triumphant

BY 1949 the tide was turning. The oldest classes of double-deckers — STs and LTs dating from 1929 — were now nearing extinction. I made my last journey in a double-deck LT — an Elmers End example — in September 1948 on route 194 from my new school, Whitgift Middle, in the centre of Croydon to our playing fields at Shirley. Elmers End garage operated nothing but LTs and thus was an early candidate for RTs. By the end of September our Wednesday- and Saturday-afternoon journeys to learn the secrets of the strange oval ball game played by public schools would be undertaken in an RT which was so new that it gave off that rich aroma of fresh paint and upholstery unique to the RT family. Who could resist such a vehicle? But I was sorry to see the end of the LT, with its six wheels (very impressive) and its variety of architectural styles, ranging from the outside-staircase versions — a

Right at the end of their careers several former Tilling STLs migrated to the 'far north' and ended their days in Country Area green livery, like STL115 seen in Watford in 1948. *Author's collection*

throwback to the horse bus — through the inevitable variations on the theme of route indicators, to the impressive-looking 'Bluebirds' which, back in 1930, had heralded the future. One achieved a sort of immortality by being driven around Brooklands race track at speeds far in excess of what were normally required of it in a Will Hay film. Neither the first nor the final versions of the LT were normally seen in Croydon, which made them more exotic, and I had to venture to Victoria to get a ride on an open staircase 38A or Mitcham for a 'Bluebird' 88 and see Dad play cricket and receive personal tuition on how to spin a googly from a former Surrey Second XI player — not that it did me much good as wicket-keeper for the 3B Second XI. My very last sight of an LT was of one of Hammersmith's heading along Buckingham Palace Road for Liverpool Street on London's most famous route, the 11.

STs too disappeared from the streets of Croydon, replaced both by RTs and by standard STLs drafted in from elsewhere. I was less put out by this, for the ST came in only one variety, and that a shortened version of the least interesting LT and minus a couple of wheels, to

Above: A rather woebegone single-deck LT based at Croydon (TC) garage waits at the Wallington terminus of the 234A in 1945. *Author's collection*

Left: No 2, London's newest tram, and Metro-Cammell-bodied RTL765 at Eltham church. *R. Hubble*

boot. It looked as if just one of each would survive in preservation, but later Prince Marshall found Tilling ST922 mouldering away in a scrapyard and had it beautifully restored. The official preserved ST was not, as it happened, ex-General but rather one from the National fleet. This was almost standard but had a smaller front indicator and looked a little odd when repainted into red and first put on display, many years later, at the Museum of British Transport in the former bus garage at Clapham. Tending to be the sort of people who go into terminal decline if, having counted nine million and three rivets, they find they are one short, some enthusiasts got very hot under the collar about this, but ST821 eventually reverted to London Transport postwar green, and peace and harmony once more reigned. Decades later, LT165 was joined by the newly rediscovered remains of a couple of single-deck versions ('Scooters') and, as I write, restoration of that belonging to the London Transport collection is almost complete.

The single-deck LTs lasted rather longer than did the double-deckers, 60 being rebuilt by Marshall in 1948/9, enabling me to ride into the rural fastness of Riddlesdown on one on Croydon's 234A route in late 1949. To all intents and purposes the ST also disappeared by the end of that year; a few just lasted into 1950, while six lowbridge examples in the Country Area

Right: It is difficult to imagine the fashionable King's Road, Chelsea, and the workaday tram co-existing, but the junction of Beaufort Street and King's Road was the terminus of the 34. After crossing Battersea Bridge its route took it through Clapham, Brixton and the Elephant & Castle before terminating back on the north bank of the Thames at Blackfriars. A typical Thompson night-time shot of an 'E1' beside the river.
D. A. Thompson

Below: An 'E1' tram and RT1147 of Croydon (TC) garage on the Embankment in September 1949.
A. W. V. Mace

Left: A contrast in styles between tram No 96, an ex-East Ham car built in 1928 to an Edwardian design, and a very Transatlantic-looking brand-new Vauxhall Wyvern and an RTL, both of 1950.

Below: ST141, one of only eight members of its class to survive beyond the beginning of 1950. All eight were lowbridge examples, and ST141 once belonged to the National Omnibus & Transport Co. Although in Country Area livery, it is seen working the Central Area 230 from Harrow Weald (HD) garage. *Author's collection*

were needed for a little while longer. A curious late phenomenon to be seen in the streets of Croydon was an ST adorned in blue and yellow, having been employed on Inter Station duties between 1943 and 1946. The last of these returned to normal duties, initially without being repainted, in 1947, when some of the Leyland 1½-decker Cubs built specifically for Inter Station work were returned from the Railway Air Service and once again ran between the main-line stations.

I know of no ST or LT which passed to new owners and was operated as a PSV (although in some cases the chassis saw further service), but the STL was virtually the first London type to go on to carry passengers after London Transport had dispensed with its services. Relatively few were fit enough so to do, but this nevertheless marked the beginning of a trend which would see ex-London buses take up work all over the world.

A curious arrival at the end of 1949 was G436. Guys, despite their poor bodywork, had impressed a number of operators which had been forced to buy the make during the war years — one thinks particularly of Southdown and Chatham & District — and they were selling well in the late 1940s. A solitary Arab, with a very powerful 10.35-litre Meadows engine and air-operated preselector gearbox, was sold to London Transport in

November 1949. It had a standard Park Royal body and looked as if it had taken a wrong turn upon delivery to Midland Red or East Kent. The intention was that a second chassis adapted to take the Park Royal or Weymann RT body, should follow it, but this never happened, and G436 remained unique in the London Transport fleet.

Remarkable survivors right through the 1940s were examples of the NS class. Of almost prehistoric aspect, these ancient objects, dating from 1923 and the link between the horse bus and the modern double-decker, had last run in passenger service in 1937. However, 12, including one single-decker, were converted to mobile canteens, in which form they popped up all over the London Transport area, being particularly useful during the war in keeping hard-pressed crews fed and watered in emergencies, when their own garage canteens were out of action. One NS was withdrawn in 1944, and most of the others had gone by the end of the 1940s, but two lasted into the 1950s. One of these was the former NS2295 (No 39H in the service fleet). I paid a visit to Chelsham garage early in 1950 to admire the new KXW-registered RTs which had just been delivered. I was particularly intrigued by the 2499-2521 series, all of which worked through Croydon, for the bus-spotters' grapevine had it that RT2500 was going to be the last RT. How wrong could we be? Parked to one side of the garage, in stark contrast to the gleaming, dark-green, state-of-the-art RTs, was an extraordinary apparition.

G436, the solitary Park Royal-bodied Guy Arab of 1949, at Peckham. *F. G. Reynolds*

Three London General NS buses, converted in 1937 to mobile canteens, awaiting disposal in 1949. From left to right are NS577, 1129 and 2322. *Alan Cross*

Painted a drab shade of leaf green, it had minimal mudguards, a radiator which was wider than it was tall, a towering driving cab much higher than the rest of the lower deck, a four-piece front window on the upper deck and many other features I associated with a long-vanished era. Just visible on the panels where 'LONDON TRANSPORT' would normally be was the legend 'STAFF CANTEEN'; below was the wording 'LONDON TRANSPORT EXECUTIVE' — there were very few NSs which lasted long enough to become part of the nationalised industry. A short while later, having defied Old Father Time for over a decade, NS2295 finally met its end and was sold to a dealer in April 1951 and broken up. Whenever I visit the London Transport Museum at Covent Garden I always take a look at the sole surviving NS (NS1995) and reflect that I came across such an antiquity which just made it into the second half of the 20th century.

Six Tilling STs were converted to mobile canteens in 1946/7, but these were only a stopgap. However, one of these — ST922 — kept going until 1955 and (as already described) was eventually preserved by Prince Marshall. Many years later, in the 1970s, it returned to passenger service, operating tourist route 100 in Central London, and lives today at Cobham, still roadworthy and often seen out and about. More permanent replacements for the NS canteens arrived in 1947/8 in the shape of purpose-built vehicles. These were based on Scammell chassis and had semi-trailer bodies built, very much in the Chiswick stylistic tradition, by Spurling of Hendon. They were hauled by petrol-engined Bedford tractor

units — one of the classic designs of all times and the most popular commercial vehicle of the early postwar years. There were 10 of these, numbered 700-9B (HLX 480, JXC 1-9). These, in turn, were withdrawn between 1959 and 1967. Bedford No 702B (trailer unit No MC11) is still with us, having passed into preservation and is yet another resident of the Cobham Bus Museum.

No fewer than 1,592 new double-deckers entered service with London Transport in 1949. Extraordinary as this total was, it would be exceeded the following year. Nevertheless 1949 is highly significant in the history of London Transport, not only for the volume of new vehicles but also for the introduction of three new varieties within the RT family.

The RT is rightly remembered as one of the all-time classic PSVs, yet two of the varieties introduced in 1949 were short-lived failures. The more unusual (and a one-off) was RTC1. Strictly speaking this wasn't a new vehicle at all, being a rebuild of war-damaged RT97, but it certainly looked completely new. Intended to be the forerunner of a class of double-deck coaches, it was a striking-looking vehicle and was tried out on a number of Green Line routes. A great deal of thought had gone into its planning. A new suspension system was fitted, lighting was by fluorescent tubes, there was air

Above: Men in long, brown mackintoshes stride purposefully across Piccadilly Circus as a Battersea-based RT on route 19 passes Eros. *Author*

Right: A graphic illustration of just how appalling the London fogs of the 1940s and '50s could be. The bus is an RTL. *London Transport*

RTC1, the handsome if unsuccessful double-deck Green Line coach, originally RT97. Although it was deemed a failure, many of its features would be incorporated in the successful Routemaster coaches of a decade later. *London Transport*

conditioning, and the 46 seats were the result of a survey of passengers' preferences. Sadly RTC1 was not a success. The suspension gave rise to many complaints, there were no overhead luggage racks, and mechanically it was not very reliable. After nine months it was relegated to bus work and was eventually withdrawn in 1953. However, it was an experiment worth carrying out, and much of the experience gained would be put to good use with the production Routemaster coaches of the 1960s.

The SRT arose from the fact that production of RT bodies was running ahead of that of chassis, it being decided that 300 of the latest prewar STL chassis should be refurbished — remember that it was the bodies which were wearing out quicker than the chassis — and fitted with RT bodies. The STL chassis in question came initially from buses of the FJJ- and FXT-registered batches; their bodies were not broken up but were transferred to earlier (mainly DLU-registered) members of the class, whose Park Royal all-metal bodies of 1937 were in a very sorry state (although, ironically, one or two of these would still be in passenger service when the last SRT was withdrawn). The problems with the SRTs soon became apparent and stemmed from the fact that they were a good deal heavier than the STL yet retained the STL engine, so that performance was sluggish. Perhaps even worse, their brakes were unreliable. Not surprisingly drivers hated them. They were kept off hilly routes, and, although their brakes were modified, the problem was never solved. The various modifications included lowering the radiator, so that, in just about

every respect, an SRT looked exactly like an RT; the only clue that it was a pussycat pretending to be a tiger was the retention of the original registration number. Latterly a few of the earlier, DLU-registered STLs were converted to SRTs, but the intended total of 300 was never reached, production ending at SRT160.

The final 1949 variation on the RT was perfectly satisfactory. The 500 Leylands intended to be RTL1-500 eventually emerged as RTWs, which, like their prewar Titan predecessors (STDs) of 1937, were entirely of Leyland manufacture. The STD was not a bad attempt at copying the contemporary STL, but the resemblance was far from perfect; with the RTW Leyland got it just about spot on. Apart from the extra 6in width it looked 98% like an RTL, inside and out. The earlier examples had the characteristic up-and-down Leyland rainstrip above the rear window, and all had black rubber-mounted route indicators, but otherwise even the most dedicated rivet-counter would have been hard-put to spot the difference. Because of their 8ft width the Metropolitan Police insisted they stay in the suburbs, like London's other eight-footers, the 'SA' and 'Q' class trolleybuses. However, they were most needed on the busiest Central London routes, where their extra width made ingress and egress that much easier. Indeed, several of the suburban routes upon which they were originally employed were just as narrow as any to be found in the City or the West End, but the ways of the Metropolitan Police in public-transport matters were always eccentric and generally backwards-looking. In 1950 it agreed to trials in Central

London, and from then on the RTW became a familiar sight in Oxford Street, around Trafalgar Square and elsewhere in the heart of the capital. However, no 8ft version of the RT was ever produced, and a number of garages had to have structural alterations before they could accommodate the RTWs.

Within the RT class itself two further variations appeared in late 1948. From the outset it was clear that production of the chassis would outstrip that of the bodies by Park Royal and Weymann, and various other builders were approached. After much negotiation, contracts were signed with Cravens of Sheffield and Saunders on the faraway Isle of Anglesey, the latter firm being yet another better known for its aircraft activities. The two took a very different approach to the task. Saunders produced a body (classified RT3/3) which was virtually pure Chiswick down to the tiniest detail; the Cravens version (RT3/4) most certainly wasn't. The first Saunders to appear locally was RT1155, which was delivered to Croydon garage in March. It had a roof-mounted number box and looked exactly like one of the final Park Royal or Weymann roofbox varieties.

The first 27 Cravens-bodied RTs went to the Country Area — the only non-Weymann RTs delivered new in green — and it was May 1949 before the first red examples arrived. These were sent to Nunhead and Elmers End garages and thus brought yet more brand-new buses to the streets of Croydon, on routes 12 and 194. The cab area was standard RT, but the rest was quite different. Perhaps the biggest variation was the five-bay window design. There was no inward taper, making the Cravens RT look rather ungainly from the front, whilst the rear was much more curvaceous than the standard version. Internally the seats and some fittings were standard; others were not. The general opinion of the bus-spotting fraternity was that they were an interesting variation but not as good as the real thing.

The Cravens RTs had fairly short lives with London Transport but were snapped up when they appeared on the second-hand market in the mid-1950s. Thirty were bought by Dundee Corporation to replace trams, the rest mostly going to independents which couldn't believe their luck in getting such beautifully maintained buses at a bargain price. The Saunders RTs were treated as totally standard. No Cravens bodies ever left the RT1402-1521 series, but Saunders bodies were readily exchanged throughout the RT fleet. None ever appeared on an RTL, but for a time the highest-numbered RT (RT4825) had a Saunders body. The very last roofbox RT in passenger service was Saunders-bodied RT1903, which was withdrawn from Battersea garage in March 1971. Examples of both Cravens and Saunders RTs have been preserved. In all there were 300 Saunders and 120 Cravens RTs.

Left: RTWs 164 and 263 pass at Kensington, proving that 8ft-wide buses could operate successfully in the heart of London. *Ian Allan Library*

Below: Close to the Bank of England, RTW47 makes its stately progress through the narrow streets of the City of London. *Alan Cross*

Right: In the postwar years Morden Northern Line station forecourt was a haunt of Daimlers from Sutton and Merton garages, but you could also be sure to see a 'prewar' RT from Putney on the 93, a route which extended deep into Country Area at Dorking, the southwestern extremity of the vast LT empire these pioneer RTs normally reached. RT71 is on a short working to Epsom. *Alan B. Cross*

Below: An official photograph of Weymann-bodied RT3066, taken before the bus entered service in 1949. *MCW*

The year 1949 was the last in which the South London tram network would remain intact, for the final demise of the London tram — or so everyone thought — would begin with the replacement of the Wandsworth and Battersea trams in the autumn of 1950. Work began in 1949 on the rebuilding or replacement of a number of tram depots.

Many consider that the summer of 1939 marked the zenith of London Transport, but an equally strong argument can be made for the final days of 1949. Huge reliance was still placed on the Executive's bus, trolleybus, tram and railway services, by Londoners and those served by the Country Area buses and Green Line in the Home Counties. Much of the ground lost

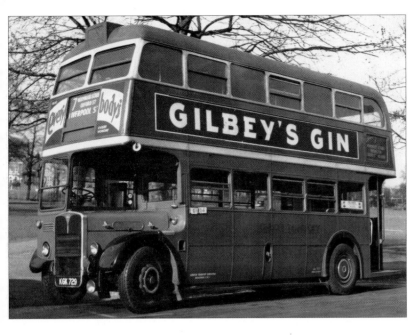

Left: Cravens RT1470 of Middle Row garage, Kensington (X), takes a breather at Acton Vale before heading back to the West End and the City in 1949. *S. L. Poole*

Below: Park Royal-bodied RTL521 at home in Barking garage before setting off on an excursion to Whipsnade Zoo. In the background is a selection of Gs and further RTLs. *D. A. Jones*

between 1939 and 1945 had been made up. The trams, seen by most (but not all) as old-fashioned and time-expired, might still have been with us, but production of the RT, built by AEC (the firm for ever associated with London Transport), and Leyland's RTL and RTW equivalents, would soon sweep them away. These classic double-deckers had already replaced much of the prewar bus fleet and by 1954 would reign supreme. The trolleybus fleet — the world's largest — had been boosted since the war, although its long-term future was already in doubt. Full employment, television and private motoring, which would have such an impact in the coming decade, were considerations for the future.

By the end of 1949 the stock totals of London Transport's enormous fleet of buses and coaches looked like this:

Trams

E1	491
E3	133
HR2	90
ME3	2
Feltham	91
Bluebird	1
TOTAL	**808**

Trolleybuses

A1/A2	10
B1/B2/B3	76
C1/C2/C3	251
D1/D2	152
E1/E2/E3	100
F1	100
H1	147
J1/J2/J3	148
K1/K2/K3	325
L1/L2/L3	172
M1	25
N1/N2	115
P1	25
Q1	77
SA1/SA2/SA3	43
X1/X2/X3/X4/X5/X6/X7	7
TOTAL	**1,773**

Buses

Double-deckers

LT	74
ST	146
STL	2,191
STD	176
B	29
D	281
G	436
RT	1,812
RTC	1
RTL	550
RTW	213
SRT	149

Single-deckers and coaches

T	451
LT	120
Q	231
LTC	24
TF	76
C	74
CR	47
TD	131
TOTAL	**7,212**

GRAND TOTAL **9,793**

Of these, the LTC class, used exclusively for private hire, and the CRs were not officially scheduled for regular service. It will be seen that the STL class was still the largest numerically, although would not be for much longer: in 1950 it would be decimated, over a thousand being taken out of service, whilst the RT/RTL/RTW classes would increase by more than 1,500.

Another view of the unique LT1131, this time in rural outer-suburban Kent. The LT class, in its various forms, would serve London Transport throughout the 1940s, the last examples surviving until 1953.
F. G. Reynolds